LEARNING TO LIVE THE GOOD LIFE

Values in Adulthood

Clive Beck

Monograph Series / 26

OISE Press

The Ontario Institute for Studies in E

The Ontario Institute for Studies in Education has three prime functions: to conduct programs of graduate study in education, to undertake research in education, and to assist in the implementation of the findings of educational studies. The Institute is a college chartered by an Act of the Ontario Legislature in 1965. It is affiliated with the University of Toronto for graduate studies purposes.

The publications program of the Institute has been established to make available information and materials arising from studies in education, to foster the spirit of critical inquiry, and to provide a forum for the exchange of ideas about education. The opinions expressed should be viewed as those of the contributors.

252 Bloor Street West
Toronto, Ontario
M5S 1V6

Canadian Cataloguing in Publication Data

Beck, Clive, 1939-
Learning to live the good life : values in adulthood

(Monograph series ; 26)
Includes bibliographical reference and index.
ISBN 0-7744-0399-3

1. Values. 2. Adulthood. I. Title. II. Series: Monograph series (Ontario Institute for Studies in Education) ; 26.

BJ1581.2.B43 1993 170 C93-094395-3

ISBN 0-7744-0399-3 Printed in Canada

1 2 3 4 5 6 KP 89 79 69 59 49 39

DEDICATION

For the students in my adult values classes who, by generously sharing their experiences and insights with me over the years, have taught me so much about how to live the good life.

Contents

ACKNOWLEDGMENTS

Apart from my students, to whom this book is dedicated, I am grateful to many friends and colleagues who gave valuable feedback on earlier drafts. I wish to mention especially Isa Aron, Donald Brundage, Barbara Burnaby, Vivian Darroch-Lozowski and Madhu Suri Prakash. They will not, of course, agree with everything that remains in this final version! I wish also to thank Beulah Worrell for her excellent word-processing, John McConnell for his crucial editing role, and my colleague Christopher Olsen for his tireless and expert help in formatting and printing the final "camera-ready" document for OISE Press.

CHAPTER 1

Introduction: Learning to Live the Good Life

Questions Everyone Is Asking

The topics of this book are, I believe, of concern to every human being. Certainly in my own case, understanding values and how they are learned was just as important growing up on a farm in remote Western Australia as it is today working as a professor in urban North America. I wanted to know then, as I do now, what is worth pursuing in life, how to figure out ("work out" we said in Australia) how to live, and where to go for extra help. And I think everyone, consciously or not, is constantly investigating these matters. We all want to make something of our lives, find "well-being" or "the good life." It's not just an interest of philosophers, educators, and other experts.

I say this partly to encourage people who aren't educators to read on. But it is crucial also for educators to see themselves as fellow learners, asking the same questions as everyone else. If they are not constantly developing their own values, they will not have much to offer others, whether students, friends, or their own children. And they will also tend to preach at others rather than learn from and with them.

Where Do Values Come From?

I believe everyone can explore value questions because *values arise within everyday life*. They don't come from an external source, and we don't need philosophers or priests to tell us what to value. Such experts can help us refine our values, but the main process of discovering and developing them is something *we* do, as individuals and in family and communal groups. (And we, in turn, can help experts refine *their* values.)

To a large extent, values are grounded in human nature. All specific values may be traced back to "basic values" which humans simply *do* pursue. Here are some examples of basic values:

survival
health
happiness
companionship
friendship
sympathy for others
helping others
self-respect
respect from others
discovery
aesthetic experience
fulfilment
freedom
a sense of meaning in life

I call these values "basic" because they are largely ends in themselves; ultimately, they are what makes life seem good and worthwhile. Together, they define well-being or the good life.

Basic values such as these are pursued by everyone. Even the humblest woman or man in the street will say: "If you're healthy and happy and have some friends, luv, that's what matters." Even where people deny that they value these things, if you follow them around for a few days you will see them eating healthy foods, doing things they enjoy, trying to find amiable companions, and so on.

While pursued by everyone, these values aren't eternal and universal in a strict sense. The precise *form* they take and the emphasis placed on each changes over time and is strongly influenced by culture. Some cultures, for example, encourage *non*-survival (that is, suicide) in certain kinds of situation; and societies vary in their conceptions of happiness and fulfilment. But whatever the form, these basic values are remarkably persistent. To a large degree, they have a life of their own, resisting attempts to stamp them out or control them completely.

People do pursue such values, then. But is that enough justification? Shouldn't there be some kind of external validation? I don't think so. I accept the "postmodern" insight that there is no overarching structure or underlying foundation to life. It is enough that this is what people seek and find satisfying and fulfilling. Of course, not everything we pursue is good: we can make mistakes in value matters. For example, I may buy a car that I don't really need or eat a kind of food that does me more harm than good. But the basic values which lie behind these actions — pleasure, health, survival, a feeling of well-being — are not in question. They are what life is all about.

Morality as a Means to the Good Life

Moral virtues, you may have noticed, are not on the above list of basic values. In my view, being moral should be seen not as an end in itself but rather as a *means* to the good life, for ourselves and others. Truthfulness and reliability, for example, are not good in themselves. Rather, they are good *insofar as* they help people live well. Clearly we sometimes have to tell a lie (a "white lie") or break a promise for the sake of people's overall well-being.

This is not a selfish or "egoistic" position. I'm not saying that morality should be treated as a means to *our* well-being as against that of other people. Rather, it is important for everyone's well-being that morality be seen in this way. Often when we break a moral rule it's to protect or help someone else, not ourselves.

Societal leaders, religious leaders, parents, and teachers so often try to convince us that moral values are ends in themselves. We are told that *it is just wrong* to resist authority, speak out against our country, be a practising homosexual, have premarital sex, talk back to our elders, not work hard at school. But we should see this as a way of imposing authority, of avoiding dialogue about just whose well-being these prohibitions serve. Certainly, such authorities don't see moral rules as absolutes for *themselves*. They are quick to tell white lies or break promises if they think the circumstances justify it. The fact that they don't want us to have the same latitude should make us wary.

Religion, Too, as a Means Rather Than an End in Itself

Though I have abandoned my own fundamentalist Baptist upbringing, and don't think there is "one true way" (how could there be when good, spiritual human beings — both religious and non-religious — follow different paths?), I believe that religious traditions and communities are often of great benefit to their adherents. I would include fundamentalist religions here; despite their drawbacks, the very sense of tradition and community they provide meets a need often felt in modern secular society. (I wrote this *before* Bill Clinton was elected as the new U.S. President, honest!)

But as with morality, so with religion, the mistake lies in seeing it as an end in itself rather than a means. The whole point of religion is to enable people to flourish, to live the good life. As Jesus said, sabbath observance was made for people, not people for sabbath observance.

To return to my own case, I would perhaps still be a Western Australian Baptist of a sort if I hadn't moved first to the wicked "Eastern States" of Australia and then to Canada. I would have probably gone to church every now and then (not twice every Sunday and another night a week as in my childhood and youth) and attended weddings, funerals, seasonal services, and so on. In many ways I miss the old community links, the sense of belonging, the utopian, spine-tingling hymns . . . my "roots." There would have been conscience pangs from time to time because of the exclusivism, sexism, and other problems of Christianity; how could I, even in a small way, identify with and lend credence to such a flawed tradition? But what tradition and community is not flawed? Certainly the academic community in which I now participate has its problems.

But even if I had in a modest way stayed with my childhood religion, I would have approached it as a means to the good life, a means to sociability, celebration, expansiveness, rather than the opposite. I would have tried to make it a work of life rather than of death (as Emile Durkheim said in talking about morality). Too often, as I was growing up, religion got in the way of human flourishing. For example, my religion at the time placed severe constraints on sexuality among young people, including "sex-related" pursuits such as dancing, movie going, and "wild" parties. As a result, while as a good farmer's boy I knew quite well how sheep and cattle mated, I had no idea how or why humans would do the same. When two older teenagers in our youth group "had to get married" because she became pregnant, I was at a loss to understand how something so much against the rules could have happened.

But, of course, that is the point. Human life keeps breaking through, despite the rules. And while rules, or at least guidelines, are often valuable, they should enhance life rather than suppress it. Perhaps those two teenagers shouldn't have been having sex when they did, especially as it led to their "having to get married." But my church's only suggestion was complete abstinence, which was obviously not realistic.

To repeat: the point of the exercise, *any* exercise, is to promote well-being, our own and other people's. No religion or morality or political system or educational institution has any business pursuing its own ends at the expense of human well-being (or the well-being of the Earth, for that matter, which is essential to human well-being). This doesn't mean that we should neglect the societal, the communal, the institutional. That was the mistake British utilitarianism led us to, resulting in today's careless mobility and lonely individualism. But it does mean that the communities and institutions we create (or re-create) must be expressly designed to promote the good life rather than push some agenda of their own.

The Rough and Tumble of Life

This sort of talk may lead to doubts and fears. How can we figure things out for ourselves, from scratch? Surely we will make mistakes. Don't we humans need the direction and security of an objective morality and a stable religion?

Well, to begin with, we don't have to start from scratch: we have thousands of years of religious and secular tradition on which to draw. And we don't have to figure things out for ourselves. We can do it with our family, friends, fellow community members, and a raft of "experts" whose ideas are conveyed to us constantly through the media. In many ways, people are less alone today in solving the problems of body, mind, and spirit than ever before in human history.

On the other hand, it must be frankly admitted that life has a "rough and tumble" quality about it. As the postmodernists have pointed out, reality is constantly changing, it is a historical process, nothing is eternal or universal except change itself. Within that process we can identify "enduring interests" (John Dewey) and "tentative frameworks" (Charles Taylor). (And I think postmodernists have often underestimated these possibilities.) But there are no absolute, unchanging realities or values. Even in religion, in the West we now have "process theology" which sees the whole of reality, including the divine, as constantly evolving. And in the East, the notion that the universe is in an endless state of flux has been widespread for millennia.

Such a view of reality, however, still leaves us with sufficient sources of direction and meaning in life. It takes some adjustment to go from finding life's direction and meaning in absolutes to finding it in processes, qualified generalizations, and basic values whose precise form keeps changing. But in my experience the shift can be made; and in a sense the new basis is more solid, since we don't have to force ourselves to believe in it and we are spared rude shocks when contrary evidence turns up. Furthermore, it is not really a completely new step, even for religious people. The comfort and security of religious belief have always been supplemented by more worldly realities. I was struck by this recently when I visited the farm where my ancestors first settled in Western Australia. At the bottom of a memorial plaque installed in honor of my great-grandparents was the inscription: "They Feared God — They Loved the Land." To these settlers, the land was perhaps as much a source of satisfaction, security, and meaning as their religion.

On the matter of making mistakes, we have to admit that this will happen. But once again, I don't see this as a problem: we already make many mistakes and yet manage. Indeed, acknowledging that we will make mistakes is of crucial importance in living the good life. In most situations we have to act on probabilities or we can't act at all. A business deal, a marriage, having a child, a career move, starting a friendship, having an operation: each of these in a particular case *may* turn out to be a mistake. We rarely know for certain that we are making the best possible decision or even a good one. However, what we can be fairly confident of is that if at every point we take the step that seems most likely to be sound, then *on balance* our life will go in a good direction. I say "fairly confident" because a continuous run of bad luck can undermine almost any way of life, no matter how careful we are. It was because of this feature of the human condition that the ancient Greeks said: Count no man happy until he is dead.

Accepting the rough and tumble of life — constant change, mistakes, uncertainty — is essential for well-being. Hankering after moral and religious absolutes is an expression of our Western perfectionism, which does so much harm. We are always searching for total security, complete happiness, perfect relationships, the final truth. What we need to recognize is that human life has never been and never will be perfect, although it can be very good. And paradoxically, it is when we stop insisting on the perfect that we are able to attain the good.

Phases of Value Development

As I have said, values are not eternal. The precise form even of basic values keeps changing; and we never solve value problems once and for all. This is partly because our cultural, economic, and ecological environment keeps changing, requiring adjustments in our way of life. But there are also changes related to age. Different phases in the life cycle require different values. For example, when in early adulthood we pass from being dependents to having children of our own, we must accept new responsibilities and take an interest in new things, such as diaper rash, infant nutrition, children's toys (often to the consternation of our child-free friends). Then later, as our children in turn leave home, we have to find new pastimes and establish new family patterns.

We should not exaggerate (as I think some phase theorists have) how general these phase changes are. For example, not everyone has children; and of those who do, different people have them at different ages, in different social, financial, and marital circumstances, and at different points in their mental and emotional development.

However, even to know, for example, that *some* people experience a heightened sense of mortality in their thirties or a sense of disillusionment about their life dreams in their forties, can help us as we approach those age periods. We can prepare for the possible crisis, either to prevent it, or to make it a positive experience, or to endure it stoically, in the knowledge that others have been through it and survived. So long as we realize that not everyone must go through the same phases or in the same way, knowledge of *typical* age patterns is very useful.

Stages of Value Development

Phases of value development, we have just seen, are age specific: in your twenties this is likely, in your thirties that may well happen, and so on (depending on your culture, gender, social class, and so on). *Stages* of value development, by contrast, are not pegged to particular ages, certainly not in adulthood. According to Lawrence Kohlberg, the guru of moral stage theory, adults in their twenties and thirties are spread in large numbers across the whole spectrum from Stage 2 ("You scratch my back and I'll scratch yours") to Stage 5 (a flexible, reflective, "post-conventional" morality).

Now, I am not at all keen on stage theories, and will spend much of my chapter on the subject (Chapter 7) trying to show that such stages don't exist. My main objection to stage theories is that they are "age-ist". While they don't tie stages to particular ages, they claim that later stages must come after — usually a long time after — earlier ones. This means that *on average* adults are morally wiser than children and older adults are morally wiser than younger adults. Such age bias supports a "holier than thou" attitude among older people and leads to all kinds of unproductive conflict between the generations.

Does this mean we can't improve in value matters as we grow older? Of course we can. Otherwise, there would be no point in the counselling, exhortation, values education, and so on, which we all assume is important. However, my view is that improvement takes place across the whole age spectrum of a society. It is just as possible — and happens just as often — among younger people as among older people.

Change and Continuity in Values

Phase and stage theories emphasize change in values. But equally common and important is continuity in values. For example, the basic values — survival, happiness, friendship, and so on — are pursued throughout life by virtually everyone, although as we have noted their *form* often changes. Also, many idiosyncratic values persist throughout life: some people are more careful than others, or more courageous, or more inquisitive, or more social, from childhood to the grave.

Self-centredness, to take a key example, normally doesn't change very much with age. In any group of ten year olds, twenty-five year olds, or fifty year olds, one sees the same spectrum from more to less self-centred individuals. There is *not* a steady shift from egocentrism in childhood to altruism in late adulthood. It is often said, for example, that adolescents are very self-centred. But in fact, they typically show great generosity toward their peers and to strangers of diverse races and cultural backgrounds, often to the chagrin of their parents who are trying to instill in them a "proper" sense of who their inner circle is.

Fiske and Chiriboga in their recent book *Change and Continuity in Adult Life* (San Francisco: Jossey-Bass) tell the story of Daphne Randall, who "spent all but the last two or three years of her life trapped in a world that demanded subservience to the needs of others. With her husband's death and the departure of her son, she suddenly gained a freedom she vigorously pursued until her untimely death" (p. 292). The authors don't say that Daphne Randall became more assertive and outgoing as she grew older: her personality didn't change in these areas. Rather, she finally gave expression to qualities which had been "submerged . . . as a result of social constraints." The moral to be drawn from this case and others is that, as values learners and teachers, we need to give attention not only to personality change but also to building the life structures that enable sound values to be expressed, values which in many cases have been part of our nature from an early age. Change in values is not always the most important consideration in promoting well-being.

Fine-Tuning What Is Already There

To summarize some of what I have said up to this point: Values are essential to living well; and because everyone wants to live well, we can be assured that people are already working steadily at developing their value system and way of life, with a view to attaining the good life for themselves and at least some others. As people grow older, their priorities shift somewhat and their values adjust to age-specific characteristics of their culture, gender, class, and so on. However, many values remain much the same, reflecting continuous features of their personality, needs, and circumstances.

One of the implications of this analysis is that the task of learning and teaching values is not to "fill empty vessels" but rather to accept and build on people's existing way of life. To me one of the most important principles of adult education (indeed of all education) is: "People aren't stupid." They have good reasons for the way they live, no matter how strange it may seem to outsiders. They already know a great deal about values and how to live well. This applies as much to Western Australian Baptists, Hindu mystics, and Californian yuppies as to anyone else: they have already carved out quite a good way of life for themselves.

When we talk of "learning to live the good life," then, and "teaching values in adulthood," it's not a matter of initiating people into an entirely new science or changing completely their current practices. In learning and teaching values the object is not to replace the strings of the violin, so to speak, or to make a G string into a D string, but rather to fine-tune the strings. The goal is to enhance what is already there rather than to replace it.

Some people, however, question the appropriateness even of fine-tuning. On the one hand, it is said that value issues are so straightforward — "we already know what is right" — that there is nothing to be learned. On the other hand, it is said that values are so complex (or subjective or relative) that there is nothing that *can* be learned — "we can never know what is right." But clearly both these views are mistaken. On the one hand, we can work to extend and refine our value system. We already know a great deal, but there is always more to learn. On the other hand, while value issues are indeed complex and subtle, they aren't beyond our abilities. We humans show a great capacity to deal with complexity, routinely making value decisions that involve weighing hundreds of considerations in a short space of time. Utilizing that capacity, we can go on to develop even more adequate values.

There is one limitation to the analogy of fine-tuning: it implies improvement, progress, achieving a *truer* note. Much of values learning, however, is concerned not with improvement but with simply "running to stay where we are." As we have seen, life keeps changing; accordingly, we must be constantly learning if we are to remain as happy, fulfilled, committed, and so on, as we previously were. Often in adult education we have placed too much emphasis on change and improvement. But just to maintain our balance in life (like the proverbial fiddler on the roof) is an achievement to be celebrated.

Approaches to Learning and Teaching Values

With respect to traditional and modern approaches to learning and teaching values, the main observation I will make (in Chapter 13) is that they have been too narrow in scope, focussing on just two or three factors when there are literally dozens to be considered. Some have stressed social inculcation or "socialization," others direct instruction in ethics, others dilemma discussion, others psychological therapy, others "values clarification," others self-directed learning. But in fact we need to combine all of these and many more into a comprehensive approach, both for our own learning and for "teaching" values to others.

We humans, like our values, are complex. If I help an old man across the street, for example, I may do so because I am in the habit of doing so, *and* because I don't want him to be hurt, *and* because my parents taught me to be polite, *and* because I like the approval of bystanders, *and* because I am committed to the idea of a community in which people help each other, *and* because I've organized my life so that I have time to do it, *and* because I have done some "values clarification" and can see that it fits into my value system, *and* because I realize that I will be infirm like that one day, *and* because my therapist has helped me overcome a fear of making a spectacle of myself. I may need all these motivations and others beside in order to do that simple thing. It is a mistake, then, to focus on just a couple of ways of trying to learn or teach appropriate behavior.

One thing I wish to stress especially is that, insofar as we try to teach values to others — students, patients, congregants, fellow community members, our own children — we should use a "dialogue" approach as much as possible. We should recognize that we can learn as much from our "students" as they can from us. Each of them has had a life-time of experience and reflection which is a great resource. Also they have distinctive needs and circumstances. If we don't take advantage of their insights, listening to them as much as they listen to us, we will miss out on a major learning opportunity for ourselves and also hinder their learning. Further, our relationship with them will not be as enjoyable and affirming as it might otherwise be.

A Plea for More Attention to Values Learning

Whatever approaches and methods we use, I feel we simply must spend more time on values learning, both in our own lives and in educational programs. While I have stressed our achievements in value matters, especially at the individual level, I believe the neglect of value inquiry in modern Western society has had very unfortunate consequences.

For most people in wealthy industrialized countries today life can be very good (*even* during a recession!). On

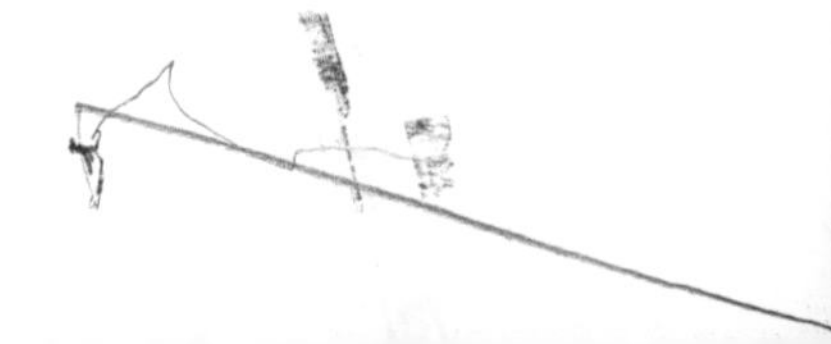

the whole we have enough food, clothing, and housing. Disease is at an all-time low and longevity continues to increase. Schooling is free. Entertainment and information come cheaply through TV, radio, films, newspapers, magazines, and books. We have a lot of freedom of thought, expression, and conduct. Compared with earlier times, public corruption is down and personal security is up. And wealthy nations have largely stopped invading each other.

And yet, ironically, so many people are still unhappy; in the midst of plenty we often feel disappointed and demoralized. In my opinion, a major reason for this is our lack of attention to values. We haven't spent enough time figuring out what is really important in life and how to achieve it. As a result, we neglect aspects of life that are fundamental to well-being, and in a desperate quest for fulfilment we consume far beyond what is necessary, with devastating effects on the environment (not to mention our own bodies).

Some may feel the answer lies in everyone going back to religion. And certainly, I believe part of the problem is that our reaction against religion in the past three centuries was so strong that we "threw out the baby with the bath water," downplaying aspects of life — ethics, "inner life," community, how to live — with which religion is associated. However, our ecological problems began while religion was still in full flood; and in the present century, conventionally religious people have lacked value direction along with the rest of us, participating in conspicuous consumption, workaholism, the decline of the extended family, and so on. The solution lies rather in *both* non-religious *and* religious communities developing more adequate value priorities. And because of the complexity of the issues, in a rapidly changing world, we require a large commitment from everyone.

* * *

As we look to the future, I wish to sound an optimistic note. The ecological situation is indeed daunting; as is the population explosion in parts of the world that can least afford it; as is the continuing and widening gap between rich and poor. But I believe that the development of more adequate values could help a great deal with these and other problems. Precisely because of our great neglect of values in the past, or an overly narrow view of them, we can expect substantial gains as we turn to comprehensive value inquiry. It won't be easy, because of the complexity I have alluded to, but there are grounds for hope. Furthermore, value inquiry is a very enjoyable pastime, and not at all expensive!

It may be felt that there is something self-indulgent about studying how to live the good life at a time when human tragedy and suffering are so widespread. Do we, who are relatively privileged, have the right to focus on this topic? However, in the first place, as we all know only too well, *everyone* experiences tragedy and suffering. "Money can't buy happiness." While there is a significant difference of degree between the situations of more and less privileged people, there is also much in common. Second, as noted earlier, deficiencies in the Western way of life are having a major impact on the global environment, so it is in everyone's interest that we "clean up" our act. And third, the principles and practice of how to live are, I believe, rather similar the world over, and we must play our part in a co-operative, global inquiry into them. *Not* to seek to learn how to live well, out of sympathy for others less fortunate, would be a nice gesture but counter-productive even for those others.

I invite you, then, to read this book. Because interests vary, you may wish to read some of the later chapters before the earlier ones. You may wish to leave out some chapters entirely. I suggest you adopt toward reading this book the approach I have advocated for values learning in general: be bold, take charge, be aware of your own distinctive needs and circumstances, be confident in your ability to figure things out, with help from your friends. These chapters are just grist for your mill.

Above all, this book should be seen not as a finished statement on the topics at hand, but as an invitation to dialogue. "Teachers and students should learn together," and certainly I have always learned as much from the "students" in my adult values classes as they have from me. I hope that together we may soon be able to go beyond the ideas and proposals of this book and gain a fuller grasp of the process and content of lifelong values learning. I would appreciate feedback from both "teachers" and "learners."

Part One:

The Nature and Source of Values

An adequate approach to values learning and education is impossible without a knowledge of the nature of values. We must know what we are trying to learn and teach, and what methods are appropriate to the subject matter. Fortunately, as noted in the Introduction, we already have considerable understanding of values as a result of life experience and everyday reflection and discussion. The following are my suggestions for "fine-tuning" that understanding.

CHAPTER 2

A General Approach to Values

I outlined my view of values in the Introduction, and will now describe it in more detail. As I said there, I believe values arise within everyday life, and everyone has considerable understanding of them already. Accordingly, while the topic is a large one on which many books have been written, I think we can make some progress even in the limited space available to us here.

The Basis of Values

Values are grounded in *well-being* or what is sometimes called "the good life." Particular actions and pursuits are good and right (if they are) because they promote well-being.[1]

Well-being or the good life involves attaining *basic values* such as survival, health, happiness, friendship, helping others, self-respect, respect from others, knowl-

1. The focus in this book will be on human well-being. The well-being of animals, plants, and even objects is also important in certain ways, but the issues in this area are too complex to be dealt with here.

edge, freedom, fulfilment, a sense of meaning in life. These values, which are largely ends in themselves, are tied to basic human desires and tendencies. They are what ultimately makes life seem good and worthwhile.

On this view, there is not just one value which is the basis of all others; rather, there is a set of basic values. Through the ages it has been suggested that life's ultimate goal is happiness, or love, or truth, or beauty, or survival. But in fact there are many values which we pursue as ends in themselves, and which together ground our value system.

As noted in the Introduction, values are neither eternal nor universal. This is especially true of specific values; but even the more general "basic values" change in their precise form over time and from individual to individual and culture to culture. Behind the common labels for basic values, then, lies considerable diversity.

The conception of values I am proposing is sometimes called "teleological," from the Greek word *telos* meaning end or goal. Objects and actions are good because they promote one or more goals. By contrast, a "deontological" approach sees goodness or rightness in the action or "duty" itself, rather than in the end(s) it serves.

Not all teleological views are the same, however. Some tend to accept what we *actually* desire and pursue, while others are more prescriptive about what we *should* seek. Aristotle, for example, stressed that we should live up to our potential nature as distinct from our present actual nature. And among the British utilitarians, while Jeremy Bentham accepted all types of pleasure, J.S. Mill said we must maximize "higher" pleasures.

The approach I am proposing is relatively non-prescriptive. The basic values listed above are chosen because they are largely what people actually desire and pursue. My attempt, then, is not to change people's basic values, but to help them see more clearly and pursue more effectively what they really want and what really brings them satisfaction.

Some persuasion usually enters in, however. As Herbert Marcuse said in *One-Dimensional Man* [2] and *An Essay on Liberation*,[3] many of our natural, biological desires — for freedom, play, beauty, tenderness, and sensuousness, for example — have to a degree been buried. "The so-called consumer economy and the politics of corporate capitalism (among other things) have created a second nature of man which ties him libidinally and aggressively to the commodity form."[4] So we must help people search for their natural satisfactions, their true sources of well-being.

But we should not exaggerate (as I think Marcuse does) how much people today have lost touch with basic values. What people actually value, at this basic level, is largely what they should value. Further, we should not "prescribe" in authoritarian manner, but rather *propose* certain values for consideration. Our approach should be dialogical and "democratic." Whatever ultimate values people pursue in the end is up to them, so long as they do not interfere unduly with other people's pursuits.[5]

A Systems Approach

Basic values together with more specific types of values — moral, social, economic, political, and so on — form a *value system* which serves well-being. Within this total system all values must be weighed against one another

2. H. Marcuse, *One-Dimensional Man* (Boston: Beacon Press, 1964), *passim*.
3. H. Marcuse, *An Essay on Liberation* (Boston: Beacon Press, 1969), *passim*.
4. *Ibid*., p. 11. Parentheses added.
5. The question of the relation between self and others, in-group and out-group, will be discussed in Chapter 5.

because all are important. There are no *absolute* values, that is, ones which should always override other values. Even basic values must be weighed against each other, and are only ends in themselves to a relative degree.

Among the categories in a value system are the following:

Basic values, such as survival, health, happiness, friendship, helping others (to an extent), self-respect, freedom, fulfilment (see list given earlier);

Spiritual values, such as awareness, breadth of outlook, integration, wonder, gratitude, hope, detachment, humility, love, gentleness;

Moral values, such as carefulness, responsibility, courage, self-control, reliability, truthfulness, honesty, fairness, unselfishness;

Social and political values, such as peace, justice, due process, tolerance, participation, co-operation, sharing, loyalty, solidarity, citizenship;

Intermediate-range values, such as fitness, sporting ability, musical appreciation, good family relationships, ability to read and write, financial security;

Specific values, such as a bicycle, a telephone, a particular friendship, a high school diploma, a political party, a particular sport.

One implication of a systems approach to values is that we often have to make exceptions to principles and rules. For example, sometimes the principle of promoting health requires us to forego certain pleasures; and on other occasions health may appropriately be sacrificed to a degree for the sake of pleasure (or art, or travel). Again, sometimes the rule of telling the truth or keeping promises may have to be set aside to protect someone from harm. While we must have good reasons for breaking such principles and rules, it is obvious there are times when it would be immoral or otherwise inappropriate to stick rigidly to a practice regardless of the consequences to the people involved.

Some principles can be made absolute by definition: for example, murder is always wrong because "murder" means "wrongful killing," and "lying" is always wrong if we mean by it "illegitimate deception." However, there are circumstances in which killing (as distinct from "murder") and deception (as distinct from "lying") are justified. We must weigh the values of preserving life and telling the truth against other relevant values within the value system. There really are, then, no absolute values.

Basic values perhaps come close to being absolutes in a sense. They are the ultimates of the value system which in the end make life worthwhile. However, as we have seen, they often change over time and place. Also, even they have to be weighed against each other: health against happiness, survival against self-respect, and so on. They are ends in themselves only to a relatively high degree, not absolutely. Further, they often serve as means as well as ends. Even happiness, the consummate end, can be a means to health, for example, or better personal relations, or survival.

Values and Society

Only individuals — not societies — can experience well-being; it's the well-being of individuals which ultimately determines what is valuable. However, as we will discuss at length in later chapters, a societal perspective is also very important.

Often individuals need the help of society, or a sub-group within it, to discover which actions will best serve well-being, for themselves and others. The traditions and ongoing value inquiry of religious groups, local communities, professional associations, and so on, provide indispensable assistance. Of course, individuals must normally be free to judge which particular action is appropriate for them in a given situation. Social rules cannot cover all the intricacies of particular cases. But equally we need the social rules to give us general direction.

Apart from receiving guidance, individuals often need encouragement and even pressure from the surrounding society in order to have the motivation to do what is best. Humans are social beings. An unfavorable social context can dissuade us from doing even what we know to be right, while a supportive community can provide a crucial push toward appropriate behavior. Obviously we must cultivate the ability to resist social pressure to some extent. But moralists have often exaggerated the degree to which such resistance is possible or even desirable.

The impact of society is not always benign. As we noted earlier, Herbert Marcuse has shown how modern industrial/consumer society has distorted our values. And school critics such as Jonathan Kozol and Michael Apple have described how ideologies from the wider community enter the school and influence both teachers and students toward inappropriate values.[6] However, even escape from influence of this kind must be achieved in large part through social means. Because we are social beings, we can only benefit to a limited degree from programs of individual teaching and inquiry. In attempting to improve individual and small-group values (including one's own), much attention must be given to modifying the structure of society and the values and ideologies found in it.

There is another way in which values and society are related. Society (or culture) to a considerable extent determines what means we employ to achieve basic values, what form our satisfactions take, what gives us meaning in life. This is the truth in the somewhat misleading statement that "values are socially constructed." While

6. J. Kozol, *The Night Is Dark and I Am Far From Home*, 3rd ed. (New York: Continuum, 1984); M. Apple, *Ideology and Curriculum*, 2nd ed. (London: Routledge and Kegan Paul, 1989).

basic values in some form are found in all societies, the means of attaining them often vary markedly from one society to another. This phenomenon we should keep constantly in mind so we don't judge negatively practices of other cultures which are very different from ours but are equally good avenues to well-being.

The Objectivity of Values

Values are objective in important ways. At the level of basic values, it is an objective question what we desire and pursue. And at more specific levels, it is an objective fact that some social arrangements and patterns of behavior promote well-being better than others. Even where what is good and right changes over time and varies from person to person — as it often does — these differences can be assessed objectively, since they depend on variations in people's actual needs and circumstances. They are not random, capricious, or merely a matter of opinion.

The fact that values are objective, however, doesn't mean that they are written in the heavens somewhere, unrelated to our nature and needs; on the contrary, they are based in life. As noted earlier, values are grounded in the desires and tendencies we actually have (or can readily come to have given our nature). At a certain level — the level of what I have called basic values — we must largely accept what we desire and pursue.

G.E. Moore, an important moral philosopher writing earlier this century, claimed that goodness is in objects regardless of their relation to human beings. Attempting to establish this point, he presented the following hypothetical example:

> Let us imagine one world exceedingly beautiful. . . . And then imagine the ugliest world you can possibly conceive. Imagine it simply one heap of filth, containing everything that is most disgusting to us.

> . . . Well . . . supposing them quite apart from any possible contemplation by human beings; still, is it irrational to hold that it is better that the beautiful world should exist than the one which is ugly? Would it not be well, in any case, to do what we could to produce it rather than the other? Certainly I cannot help thinking that it would . . . .[7]

However, if by definition there is no possibility of beings ever coming in contact with these worlds, it is difficult to see why it matters whether the ugly or the beautiful one exists. While values are objective, then, they are not objective in Moore's sense. Something is good only if it is (objectively) connected to the fulfilment of basic values.[8]

It might be comforting in some ways to think that what is good and bad, right and wrong is "out there," objectively, unaffected by need, temperament, and circumstance. There is today a nostalgia for a greater degree of fixity and certainty, of a kind that is thought to have existed at some time in the past. But on the one hand, we easily forget that many people in the past found moral fixity stifling and oppressive. On the other hand, as I said in the Introduction, ideals such as happiness, friendship, knowledge, freedom, fulfilment — basic values — can become a source of security and comfort for people, even if they are not absolutes in the strict sense. A value system with such a basis may, once we become used to it, prove solid and permanent enough; and it has the added advantages of flexibility and natural appeal.

7. G. E. Moore, *Principia Ethica* (Cambridge: Cambridge University Press, 1903), pp. 83-84.

8. Of course, something might be good from the point of view of non-human beings, such as animals. But then in assessing the implications of this fact for human morality — how it should affect our attitudes and behavior — we must consider it in terms of the basic values of humans.

Are Values Relative?

It is sometimes said that values are just a matter of personal taste or opinion; or that they are culturally relative, varying purely arbitrarily from one community to another. On the account I have given, however, values aren't relative in this sense. They are grounded in objectively identifiable basic values, and what is right and good depends objectively on what serves these values. Individuals and groups don't make something good simply by believing it to be valuable, although that may be *part* of the story.

This means that it is possible to make *mistakes* in value matters, since we may be mistaken about what we really want or what will lead to our well-being or the well-being of others. It also means that we can study values systematically, finding out what constitutes well-being and what are effective ways to achieve it. We can even engage in "culture criticism," assessing the strengths and weaknesses of the values of different communities.

We must be careful, however, in concluding how other individuals and communities should live. While the questions are objective, it is not easy for outsiders to know all the relevant facts. Study must be conducted in an interactive or "dialogical" manner, ideas being developed jointly with the people concerned. It is especially important to see that, as noted earlier, there are often several equally good ways to achieve the same ends, and our favorite way of doing things may not be any better than the way chosen by other individuals or groups.

In modern times, the scientific study of so-called "primitive" cultures by anthropologists has been seen as giving support to value relativism. It is thought that the great diversity of values over time and around the world shows that values are relative. This issue has been discussed in a helpful manner by sociologist and philosopher

Morris Ginsberg who approaches it from two main directions.

On the one hand, Ginsberg maintains that the extent of the diversity of values has been greatly exaggerated. He says:

> . . . amidst variations moral codes everywhere exhibit striking similarities in essentials. . . .
>
> . . . Relativists generally stress the great diversity of morals. Yet the similarity is far greater. Westermarck — himself, be it noted, a relativist — concluded on the basis of his elaborate survey that "the moral rules laid down by the customs of savage (*sic*) peoples . . . in a very large measure resemble the rules of civilized (*sic*) nations" (Westermarck 1932, p. 197), and, so far as I can judge, later anthropological work strongly confirms his conclusion. The higher (*sic*) religions converge in their teaching of the inward nature of morality and the universality of love and its obligations. The philosophers, after the manner of their trade, emphasize their differences from each other. But in their accounts of the good . . . they move within a restricted circle of ideas — happiness, wisdom, virtue, fulfilment. These are, except on superficial analysis, interrelated, and, taking large stretches of social life, none can be attained or maintained without the others.[9]

Ginsberg's other main point is that where moral differences between people *do* exist, these can be explained without taking a relativist position. In some cases differences in circumstances call for different behavior patterns

9. M. Ginsberg, *On the Diversity of Morals* (London: Heinemann, 1956), pp. 110 and 124.

and social arrangements; and in other instances communities simply have different (but equally good) means to the same ends. Yet again, sometimes people make mistakes in value matters, and so have a different (and less satisfactory) approach in a particular value area. But variety arising out of mistakes doesn't mean that values are relative; on the contrary, if mistakes are possible, the questions must be objective.

According to Ginsberg, "there is no necessary connexion between the diversity and the relativity of morals." He says that this is clear if we distinguish two different senses of the term "ethical relativity."

> Ethical relativity may mean, in the first place, that moral value is relative to the subject asserting it or to the type of society in which it is commonly asserted. . . . [T]he implication is that there is no rational way of deciding between differing moral judgments and, indeed, that the distinction between true and false does not properly apply to them. But sometimes ethical relativity is used in another and very different sense to imply that what is right in one set of conditions may be wrong in another set of conditions, or to put it another way, that in estimating the moral quality of an act the circumstances or situation in which it occurs must be taken into consideration. "Relative" in this sense means related to surrounding conditions, and carries with it no necessary reference to subjectivity, or to the mental make-up of the person or persons judging. The two meanings are frequently confused when morality is said to be relative, and it will be readily seen that in so far as variations in moral judgment are due to differences in the circumstances or to differences in the moral import of acts under different circumstances, they cannot be used

in support of ethical relativity in the sense of ethical subjectivity.[10]

While I have referred to Ginsberg at length, I don't agree with his position entirely. Most notably, he has a notion of "higher" and "lower" religions and more and less developed societies which I would reject. Although it is true that communities make mistakes in particular areas, it has not been shown that some religions and cultures are *in general* morally superior to others. Theoretically this is possible, but the specific assumptions Ginsberg makes — that modern Western societies are superior to earlier ones, and that the "great" religions are better than "primitive" ones — are highly questionable. This does not detract, however, from his compelling arguments against value relativism. Indeed, the fact that there can be meaningful disagreement over the merits of various cultures supports the non-relativist position.

Respect for Rules

People often value rules for their own sake. Part of their motivation for being truthful, self-disciplined, or hard-working, for example, lies not in the consequences of this behavior but in a direct prizing of these virtues. As noted earlier, this is a "deontological" outlook, where people focus on right actions rather than the ends they serve. Probably all of us do this to some extent, no matter how hard we try to keep our eyes on more ultimate goals. Part of the reason, perhaps, is that society often rewards "right" behavior regardless of its effects.

In proposing a goal-oriented approach to values, I do not wish to reject respect for rules entirely. It is legitimate to have a direct attachment to honesty, loyalty, fairness, and so on, to a degree. Indeed, such respect may be an

10. *Ibid.*, pp. 99-100.

important motivating factor which helps us behave appropriately in many situations. However, problems arise when we focus *completely* on rules and disregard consequences. Immanuel Kant said, for example, that we should not lie even to a murderer who asks us where his potential victim is hiding. Such extreme respect for rules in fact subverts true moral responsibility, the ultimate goal of which is to help people and avoid harming them.

There is a paradox here. The ultimate purpose of values is to promote well-being; but in order to do so, we must acquire *some* direct affection for the rules and virtues which serve this end. (In a similar way, as Aristotle noted, we must acquire certain habits in order to be moral, even though the purpose of morality is to attain the good life, not to give expression to our habits.) The resolution of the paradox lies in keeping our respect for rules in check by reflecting frequently on the ends they serve. In this way we will be able to express our commitment to rules but also, where necessary, set them aside. We will have a tendency to behave in a certain way, but will do so in an appropriate manner and on appropriate occasions.

Direct affection for rules doubtless leads to harm from time to time; but without it, people might have even more difficulty than at present in acting appropriately. We should try to achieve the balance of motivational factors — intrinsic and extrinsic — which most promotes well-being: our own and that of others. In developing an approach to morality we should take insights from moral psychology — about what stimulates people to act in certain ways — and not focus only on ends.

Conclusion

The purpose of this chapter has been to show that the ultimate goal of values is well-being, or the good life, and to present some of the implications of this view. This leaves unaddressed an important issue, namely, how to choose between oneself and others, and between one's inner group and various other people in the world. Showing that the goal of values is well-being does not answer the crucial question: *Whose* well-being? This issue will be discussed at length in Chapter 5. Meanwhile we must look first at the nature of *moral* values, and then at the relation between values and religion.

CHAPTER 3

Moral Values

Moral values need special attention not so much because they are unique as because they have been *thought* to be unique. In fact, they come under the general account of values given in Chapter 2. They have some distinctive features but are not as different as has been claimed.

What Is Morality?

Moral values, like all other values, are concerned with promoting well-being or the good life. However, morality focusses on a particular *sub-set* of values, perhaps best described by referring to a list of moral virtues: carefulness, responsibility, courage, self-control, reliability, truthfulness, honesty, fairness, unselfishness, and so on. To be moral is to have qualities of this kind.

But while we quickly recognize the above as typical moral characteristics, the question naturally arises: *Why* do these form a distinctive set? What differentiates moral values and virtues from non-moral ones?

Over the centuries, there have been many theories of what is special about morality. It has been said, for example, that moral values have nothing to do with prudence, with what is useful. Again, it has been suggested that morality is concerned only with our duties to others and not with our own well-being. Yet again, it has been claimed that morality is distinctive in that it has nothing to do with the satisfaction of desire: moral duty is an autonomous, purely rational element in human life.

However, most attempts to explain what is distinctive about morality have, in my view, been unsuccessful. For example, the first two theories mentioned above must be rejected because they simply don't fit with what we know about moral virtues. The moral virtues of carefulness and self-control, for example, clearly have great prudential value and are of importance in managing one's own affairs as well as in helping others. Robinson Crusoe, alone on his island, had to be careful (for example, in maintaining a calendar) and self-controlled (for example, in planting some of the grain he had salvaged instead of eating it all) in order to survive and make a tolerable existence for himself. In behaving as he did, he was showing moral character.

The third account of moral distinctiveness noted above must also be rejected, for reasons we will explore in the next section. Briefly put, the idea that morality is desire-free leaves unexplained how moral behavior is possible at all; and it ignores those obvious cases of exemplary moral action which arise out of a passionate concern for the well-being of others.

The view of the distinctiveness of moral values I wish to propose is that morality is typically (though not always) concerned with *overcoming inner conflict* or with *making an effort* to do something we might not otherwise do. Courage, for example, involves taking a stand despite fears which might well have led us to back down; unselfishness is shown when we give to someone else something we would have been glad to keep for ourselves; and reliability is exhibited when we make an effort to keep a promise despite desires to do other things. By contrast, desirable non-moral traits such as an inquiring mind and a sense of humor, to the extent that people have them, seem to come more "naturally" and easily. Conflict and effort are not involved to the same degree or in the same way.

Conflict and special effort are not *always* present in moral behavior. Indeed, it might seem that in the ideal case, people are "naturally" and spontaneously courageous, responsible, and unselfish. While some would argue that such people are less moral than those who have to struggle, it would be outrageous to suggest that they are not moral at all, just because it comes relatively easily to them. Conflict and effort, then, are *typical* features of morality and help define the moral domain, but are not found in every moral action.

This account of what is distinctive about moral values helps explain the common conception of morality as concerned with the temptations of power, sex, alcohol, and the like, and with the exercise of "will power" and "moral fibre" in resisting such temptations. Although this is a caricature of morality, like most caricatures it contains some truth. Further, this account helps clarify why praise, blame, and social sanctions are especially prominent in moral contexts. These are aimed at supporting people in an inner struggle which they could well lose without outside help.

We might note in closing this section that some writers define morality very broadly, as all or most of a person's values rather than a special sub-set. While for practical reasons I have not taken this route, choosing to keep closer to ordinary usage, I am not strongly opposed to it. In the end, as has been said, it doesn't matter what you say so long as people know what you mean. If a broadening of the concept of morality could lead to greater integration of the value domain, focussed on the purpose of promoting well-being, that would be all to the good. In the present book, however, I will speak of morals as a sub-category of values, contributing along with other types of values to well-being but having within that enterprise a somewhat specialized focus.[1]

Morality and the Will

While morality often involves inner conflict and exercise of the will, the role of the will in enabling people to be moral has been greatly exaggerated. Many philosophers (most notably Immanuel Kant) have claimed that moral behavior differs from other forms of behavior in that it is unconnected with desire: truly moral action springs from a desire-free good will guided by a special faculty of moral reason. Even the desire to help others is not part of our motivation in a moral act.

The main problem with this view is that the human will, conceived as a desire-free inner force, is quite weak (if indeed it exists at all). Without appropriate desires, attitudes, habits, hopes, fears, and enabling circumstances, people are seldom able to do what they judge to be right. The will to do it, alone, is not sufficient.

It is perhaps true that humans can, at times, simply *opt* for this or that action without desire or emotion. Existentialist writers have celebrated this capacity, and it is also reflected in Richard Hare's notion of "decisions of principle," basic choices which set the direction of our moral life.[2] However, this kind of minimal, passionless choice

1. We might note also that some writers make a distinction between "morals" and "ethics." Once again, while such a distinction can sometimes be useful, I have decided to go with the more popular usage, according to which a person's morals and ethics are much the same thing. (I am not speaking here of ethics in the sense of a field of inquiry or course study.)

2. R. M. Hare, *The Language of Morals* (Oxford: Oxford University Press, 1952), especially Ch. 4.

is hardly appropriate as the centrepiece of morality. On the one hand, as we have noted, it is rarely sufficient to produce moral action. And on the other hand, most moral actions are obviously performed out of a strong and worthy *desire* to help others or achieve a personal goal.

Because the will has so little power in itself, those who emphasize its role seem forced toward either rationalism ("it is reason which drives us") or supernaturalism ("a divine spirit enables us"). But why must we adopt either of these problematic positions in moral matters? Why not simply accept that moral behavior, like other forms of behavior, is usually the product of a multiplicity of desires, dispositions, attitudes, habits, and response patterns? Rationalists and supernaturalists (in moral matters) place morality on a pedestal, above our lower natures. But this introduces a questionable dualism in human psychology. Further, the history of humankind suggests that we have been led astray by our minds and spirits at least as often as by our desires and dispositions.

One might, of course, attempt to resolve the problem by redefining "the will" to include the totality of personal components — reason, spirit, desires, habits, and so on — which lead to action, moral or otherwise. This has much to recommend it, since the notion of the will as a mysterious inner force poses many problems. However, such a redefinition would be a confusing departure from the ordinary use of the word "will." Also, it would do nothing to save the concept of moral behavior as desire-free, since desire and other everyday components of motivation would be incorporated into the concept of moral action.

Moral Motivation

If moral action is not to be explained simply in terms of the will, what is it that enables people to be moral? As noted in previous sections, moral behavior typically involves a *range* of sources of motivation rather than a single one.

Emotions such as the following play an important activating role in moral behavior:

affection	indignation
love	pride
pity	anger
shame	fear

The excitement associated with these emotions often gives part of the energy that makes moral behavior possible. While we may, for example, be guided by the principle of kindness to others, a surge of affection or pity may provide the additional "push" we need in order to follow the principle on a given occasion.

Dispositions also play an important part in moral motivation. Here are some examples:

punctuality	carefulness
reliability	thoughtfulness
honesty	temperance
fairness	frankness

Emotions are often also involved in dispositions such as these: we may be honest on a particular occasion partly out of fear of being caught. However, we frequently exercise a disposition without becoming emotional in any obvious way. The behavior has become part of our life pattern.

Ideas are also crucial to moral action. We may include here the following:

beliefs	reasons
concepts	outlooks
principles	ideals

One cannot, of course, separate ideas from emotions and dispositions, since it is the way we see a situation and its likely consequences that evokes emotions and triggers the expression of dispositions; and ideas by themselves seldom (if ever) account for behavior. But it is important not to underestimate the role of ideas.

Habits and reflexes are important "semi-automatic mechanisms" in moral action. They are major components within emotions, dispositions, and thought patterns. It is impossible to scan all our moral thought and behavior all the time. Some mechanisms must function more or less by themselves, with little or no conscious attention. (We should, however, review them from time to time to ensure that they are still working in a sound direction.)

Intuitions and conscience feelings are another set of semi-automatic components which help carry moral behavior through to completion. They are important when we don't have time for fuller consideration of a moral choice; and they may also stimulate more adequate consideration of our actions by giving us a vague sense that "something is wrong" or "something should be done." We must not absolutize the promptings of intuition and conscience: they can be mistaken and lead us astray just as easily as our more explicit attitudes and ideas. But equally they should not be dismissed as irrational and irrelevant.

Enabling circumstances have in modern times been perhaps the most overlooked component in the moral life. It is commonly suggested that a truly moral person can do what is right regardless of the situation, and difficult circumstances should not be avoided since they test and refine our morality. But the impact of context — including social context — on human behavior is a fact of life which must be taken into account. We must as far as possible choose or structure our environment deliberately so that we are able to do what we know and feel to be right.

In emphasizing semi-automatic mechanisms and enabling circumstances I don't wish to suggest that we should just do "what comes naturally." We have a responsibility to try to be moral even when our reflexes fail us and circumstances are difficult. Trying and struggling, as we saw earlier, are part of what morality is about. However, we should not be too optimistic about success in such situations, or feel unduly guilty if we fail. What is implied by this analysis is that, being human, we must take long-range steps, restructuring our personal and social reality as far as possible so that we can act morally. It is in restructuring of this kind that much of our moral responsibility lies, rather than in succeeding as rugged individuals by pure acts of will.

"Mixed Motives" and Multiple Motives

We have seen that the motivational basis of morality is complex. There are many considerations to be weighed in arriving at a moral decision; and many different components in the human psyche must work together if moral action is to take place.

In other words, being moral requires "multiple motivation." In order to make a sound moral choice we must give consideration to a range of goals, both general and specific. And in order to have the motivation to act morally, we must be propelled by a diversity of forces, both internal and external.

This view runs counter to much traditional moral instruction, which has warned us against having "mixed motives" and exhorted us to act with "singleness of purpose." But while having a mixture of motives is indeed wrong if one of the component motives is inappropriate, often the teaching has been *simply* against mixing moral and non-moral considerations, for example, honesty and self-preservation. Such a mixture has been seen as reducing or even completely undermining the goodness of an action. However, this is an unfortunate approach to morality, since it frequently results in our having insufficient motivation to do what is morally right. Further, even if we *are* able to do what we think is *morally* right without taking account of "non-moral" considerations, we may in fact do something which is wrong from a general life perspective.

The distinction between a good moral action and a good non-moral action is one of degree. It simply draws attention to the central focus of the action. In fact, as we saw in earlier sections, a moral action must take account of — and give due weight to — non-moral considerations if it is to be justifiable. Morality is not an autonomous domain which should override other values. Those who call for "pure" moral actions are ignoring this essential feature of human decision-making.

Another way of putting this point is to say that *all decisions are life decisions*. We must avoid thinking simply in terms of a single value area, such as morality. Whenever we act, all relevant considerations must be taken into account. Of course, we often talk of "moral decisions," "political decisions," "economic decisions," and so on; but this is a matter of convenience (somewhat like naming an iceberg by reference to that small part of it which is above the water). It serves to draw attention to the fact that the decisions involve moral, political, or economic considerations; or to emphasize that they have a distinctively large moral, political, or economic component. It doesn't mean that the decisions are exclusively or even mainly moral, political, or economic.

A *degree* of "single-mindedness" can have advantages in some situations. It can on occasion help us to act with style and effectiveness, uninterrupted by the weighing of other considerations; or help us to achieve a particularly important goal. However, very often the opposite is the case: style and effectiveness may be reduced by lack of awareness of the diversity of elements in a situation; and single-minded pursuit of a goal may wreak havoc in our life and in the lives of others. Breadth of outlook is normally essential to sound choice and action.

Blame and Evil

According to a traditional view of morality, we are to be blamed and should have a strong sense of shame and guilt when we act immorally. On this view, the two main elements in moral action are knowledge and the will. Moral knowledge may be acquired rather easily, through intuition or simple deduction, or by being taught a handful of straightforward moral principles and rules; and the will is set in motion through simple choice. So people who act immorally have no excuse. If they don't know what is right it is because they have wilfully refused to see or hear the obvious. And if, knowing what is right, they don't do it, this is a clear sign of blameworthiness since they could so easily have done it just by an act of will. Immorality, then, is due not to the difficulty of the task but to "hardness of heart" or "evil within us."

By contrast, the approach to morality I am proposing reduces the emphasis on blame and guilt (while not eliminating it entirely). It sees people's immorality as in part a problem for *them*, something which reduces their well-being. They are *unfortunate* (or, as the ancient Greeks said, *not blessed*) in lacking the knowledge and motivation to do what is best for them. This approach also stresses the difficulty people encounter in acting morally. There are many external factors which are largely beyond their control, at least in the short-run; and within themselves a long, painstaking process is involved in building up the insight and motivational structure needed for a higher level of morality.

This view of blame and culpability leads to a rather different conception of so-called "evil" (or "sin"). Dismissing people as "evil" is a questionable practice anyway, since they often have good reasons for their actions which we simply do not understand. (Think of Sadaam Hussein and the Iraqi Gulf war, for example, in our day.) And even where they do behave wrongly in some objective sense, we should ask ourselves whether in general they are more immoral than we are. ("Let those who are without sin cast the first stone.") Describing other people as evil is often just an easy way to boost our own ideology and further our own ends, as the history of world conquest has shown.

But an additional reason for avoiding talk of "evil people" flows from our discussion in this chapter. If individuals who are acting wrongly are actually hurting themselves (as is often the case), they are to be seen as unfortunate rather than evil, and pitied and helped rather than cursed. And if they are harming (or not helping) others not out of "hardness of heart" but because they are genuinely confused about what is right or because, sensing what is probably right, they find they cannot do it, the notion that they are "evil" (and in general more evil than ourselves) loses much of its force.

The idea of evil in the modern West has strong links with the ideology of individualism. Individuals are thought to have complete control over their own destiny and behavior. Accordingly, they are fully accountable if they fall short. But in fact, as noted in the previous chapter, humans are social beings who have only a limited capacity to rise above the level of their society. To a large extent it is a whole society — and, increasingly, a whole global community — which falls short, carrying individuals with it. As Gregory Baum has said, we in the West must return to the ancient concept of "social sin," that is, of "injustices and dehumanizing trends built into the various institutions — social, political, economic, religious, and others — which embody people's collective life."[3] As in biblical times, so today, individual "prophets" and "saints" emerge from time to time who are able to stand to a degree outside the prevailing culture in both thought and behavior. But this is an unusual capacity which serves a specific function and is not to be expected or even desired in the general population. Indeed a community would not work well if it was composed entirely of extreme solitaries of this kind.

Not that individuals are to be excused entirely. We all have some ability to choose better alternatives, for ourselves and others; and in the long term we can make significant progress even within a defective social system. But this leads only to a distinction of degree between somewhat more and somewhat less moral individuals. It does not justify a sharp dichotomy between good and evil people.

3. G. Baum, *Religion and Alienation* (New York: Paulist Press, 1975), pp. 197-202.

CHAPTER 4

Values and Religion

Many people believe religion is a uniquely rich source of ideas about values. But if questions of good and bad, right and wrong can be answered by reference to well-being or the good life, as described in Chapters 2 and 3, do we really need religion? In this chapter I will argue that while religion in the popular sense is not necessary for everyone, it is an important source of values for *some* people. Further, I will try to show that there is a very broad sense of "religion" in which *everyone* must be religious in order to have sound values.

What Is Religion?

A distinction may be drawn between religion in the "popular" sense and religion in the "broad" sense. Beginning with the popular sense, most people in the West mean by religion a phenomenon which involves some or all of the following: belief in the supernatural, belief in providence, commitment to a (religious) tradition and community, practice of certain rituals, interest in profound experiences, acceptance of a particular world view and ethical system, and preoccupation with the "large questions" of life — the nature and origin of the universe, human origins and destiny, the causes of suffering, the nature of evil, and so on. Not all of these features are essential in every case, but several must be present; and belief in a supernatural, providential order seems to be especially important.

In addition to this popular sense of religion, I wish to propose a broad usage. In the broad sense, a person may be religious without believing in "God" or "the divine" or a supernatural, providential order, and without belonging to a particular religious tradition and community or engaging in distinctively religious rituals. Religious people in the broad sense (and everyone is at least somewhat religious in this sense) embrace a set of ideas and way of life tied to a comprehensive world view and conception of what is ultimately important in life. They participate in various traditions and one or more communities, and have certain ritual-like practices expressive of their world view and values. In a sense, they even accept the "transcendent": they are open to phenomena and ideals which extend beyond their present knowledge and attainments and surprise and challenge them. They do not accept the "ineffable," the radically "other"; but they believe in the "something more," that which lies beyond domesticated reality while being continuous with it.

Religion in the broad sense is similar to what Wilfred Cantwell Smith and, following him, James Fowler have referred to as "faith" (also in a broad sense). Smith talks of faith in terms of the "totality" of people's response to religious symbols, "affecting their relation not only to those symbols but to themselves, to their fellows, and to the stars."[1] And Fowler, claiming to follow Smith, says:

> Faith is a person's or group's way of moving into the force field of life. It is our way of finding coherence in and giving meaning to the multiple forces and relations that make up our lives . . . . Whether we become nonbelievers, agnostics or atheists, we are concerned with how to put our lives together and with what will make life worth living.[2]

Religion, Basic Values, and the Good Life

Using the above definitions, we can look at the relation between religion, values, and human well-being. Beginning with *religion in the popular sense,* not everyone needs to be religious (in this sense) in order to live appropriately and well. There are many examples of people who do not believe in the supernatural or participate in a traditional religious community but who nevertheless live lives of outstanding goodness and fulfilment.

However, many individuals and groups *do* need to be religious in the popular sense in order to have sound values. *The fact that religion is not necessary for everyone does not mean that it is not necessary for anyone.* To draw an analogy, just because some people do not need to marry and have children in order to live a fulfilled life, we cannot argue that no one needs to marry and have

1. W.C. Smith, "Philosophia, as One of the Religious Traditions of Humankind," in *Différences, Valeurs, Hiérarchie: Textes Offerts à Louis Dumont,* ed. Claude Galey (Paris: Editions de l'Ecole des Hautes Etudes, 1984), p. 265.
2. J. Fowler, *Stages of Faith* (New York: Harper and Row, 1981), pp. 4-5.

children in order to be fulfilled. People's background, circumstances, and needs vary.

French sociologist Emile Durkheim was a staunch opponent of religion, and suggested replacing the authority of the Catholic religion in France with the authority of the state. Nevertheless, he maintained that the church had played an important role in French society, and stressed that one should not set it aside without putting something in its place. He said:

> . . . due to the close bond established historically between morality and religion, we can anticipate . . . that if we begin to eliminate everything religious from the traditional system without providing any substitute, we run the risk of also eliminating essential moral ideas and sentiments.[3]

Durkheim's point about moral values can be made about values in general. For many people, religion is an important mediator of a satisfactory way of life. If they were to lose their religious faith, their whole way of life would be negatively affected in the short run and perhaps permanently.

Religion (in the popular sense) helps many people achieve basic values: for example, inner peace, happiness, interpersonal harmony, companionship, a sense of belonging, wisdom, a sense of meaning in life. Religion has not always promoted these values very well: better and worse forms of a religion emerge over time. But the same may be said of non-religious traditions; and it is clear that religion has often supported a generally good way of life, well supplied with basic values.

Perhaps some people who are at present religious should give up their religion and look to non-religious

3. E. Durkheim, *Moral Education* (New York: The Free Press, 1973), p. 19.

sources for the support they need. Many have done so in the past. However, we must be aware of the possible cost to ourselves and others close to us of such a break with our childhood tradition and community. Further, we must reflect on our reasons for taking such a step. If it is because we think religion (in the popular sense) *always* undermines the good life, this is simply false. Religion can help make a good life possible.

While religion can have an important role in human life, however, not just any *form* of religion will do. If a religion is seriously undermining basic values for particular individuals and groups, it should be rejected in that form. Religion was never meant to lead to unhappiness, disharmony, loneliness, and the like. It should bring *salvation* to people, not deprivation. And a good definition of salvation is: *that state of life which brings well-being to oneself and others in this life and (for believers) in the next.* Sometimes salvation is defined in purely negative terms, as a saving *from* evil ways and a sorry end. But there must be a positive account of what people are saved *for.* Appeal to basic values, then, is a double-edged sword. It enables us both to show the value of religion (for some people) and to reject some elements of religion because they do not lead to salvation, in this positive sense.

So far in this section we have been looking at the role of religion in the popular sense in promoting well-being or basic values. However, *religion in the broad sense* can also promote well-being, and in essentially the same manner. By giving people a world view, way of life, set of traditions, and pattern of relationships, religion in this sense can provide a framework within which basic values may be attained.

We must have elements of a religious type in our life in order to live well. Values alone are not enough. But religion or "faith" of the kind Smith and Fowler describe, which is not necessarily religious in the traditional sense, can supply these additional elements. For example, general ideas about the interdependence of human beings and the importance of community can afford some of the "metaphysical underpinnings" needed in developing values of friendship and love. Again, in deciding what value to place on life, whether human or non-human, we can draw on broad conceptions of the nature of the universe, the place of various life forms in the scheme of things, and the relative value of domination and preservation, exploitation and protection. In ways such as these, religion in the broad sense can provide a basis for well-being and "salvation."

Religion and Spirituality

One group of values which have traditionally been associated with religion are what we might call "spiritual" values. By spiritual virtues or characteristics I mean ones such as the following: awareness, breadth of outlook, a holistic outlook, integration, wonder, gratitude, hope, courage, energy, detachment, acceptance, love, gentleness. Obviously these overlap considerably with other categories of value — moral, social, and intellectual, for example — but they have a distinctive focus: they are especially strongly related to our inner being or "spirit."

Spiritual characteristics are clearly valuable. For example, awareness or insight is essential in enabling us to lead our own lives well and relate appropriately to other people and to the environment. A sense of wonder adds excitement to life and also gives us an openness to new possibilities. Hope and courage support a positive attitude toward life and enable us to keep going under difficult circumstances. Acceptance and detachment help us to adjust to certain unavoidable aspects of life with good grace, and also to act with balance and timing. And love and gentleness are crucial to good relationships with other people and the ecosphere.

Traditionally, people have often seen a necessary connection between religion in the popular sense and spirituality. They have used terms such as "the spirit world" and "the spiritual domain" to refer to a separate, supernatural realm, and a "spiritual" person has been understood as someone who participates in and is affected by this realm. Spirituality has been thought to be achieved through "divine indwelling," that is, through the action of the supernatural order in the religious person.

It is apparent, however, that one does not have to be religious in the popular sense in order to be spiritual. Qualities of awareness, integration, courage, love, and gentleness are as common among atheists as among believers. And this is not surprising when one recognizes the natural processes at work in producing spiritual traits. Like moral virtues, as described in the preceding chapter, spiritual characteristics are grounded in insights, attitudes, desires, and dispositions which are available to religious and non-religious people alike.

But while religious people should give up their exclusivist claims to spirituality, non-religious people (in the popular sense) should acknowledge more explicitly than they often do the importance of spiritual qualities and the outlooks and ways of life which foster them. Further, it should be recognized that in the broad sense of religion outlined earlier, people must be religious in order to be spiritual. If they are to have these highly prized spiritual virtues, they must develop world views, relationships, attitudes, and practices which, if not religious in the popular sense, are of a religious type.

"Non-Religious" People Can Be Moral

One implication of what I have been saying is that people who are "non-religious" (in the popular sense) can be good, moral people. They need not be dismissed as "sinners," "wicked," "evil-doers" as has been common practice in the past. They are on average as concerned as religious people to live a good life and are as capable of doing so.

Durkheim, as we saw earlier, maintained that something like religion is necessary if non-religious people are to be moral. He felt that if commitment to God is abandoned, it must be replaced by commitment to something larger than ourselves, such as society, if morality is to remain intact. However, he did not believe that religion in the traditional sense was necessary for morality, and indeed saw certain advantages in a non-religious approach.

It is of course necessary for non-religious people, in developing their morality, to tap into the insights of certain traditions and communities, just as religious people draw on their religious tradition and community. It is important not to attempt to "go it alone" in moral matters. However, the traditions and communities one utilizes need not be religious in the usual sense. Further, it is possible to draw on the wisdom traditions of various religions — as Westerners, for example, are doing increasingly today with Eastern religions — while maintaining one's identity as a non-religious person.

Do non-religious people have sufficient incentive to be moral? They may see morality as promoting well-being, but is that enough? Do they need supplementary motivation such as a desire to do God's will, or a sense that the divine order will reward them (in this life and the next) if they are good or punish them if they are bad? Religions, especially in the West, have traditionally emphasized motivation of these kinds. Does it not make a difference?

Increasingly, today, even religious people are questioning motives such as these for being moral. They feel that such motivation doesn't work well and is often difficult to justify. People should be moral because they see the purpose of it, the good it brings to people. Moral conduct may be what God wills, but *why* does God will it? We need to discover that, and then act morally for those very reasons, in concert with God, so to speak, rather than out of obedience and fear of punishment. God or the gods may have a plan for the universe which includes moral conduct; but that should be our plan, too, reflectively adopted for good reasons, rather than something external to us. Viewed in this way, religious and non-religious people have the same level of motivation to be moral. A conception of a larger "plan" or cause in which we are participants is often important for moral action, but we may have such a conception without being religious (in the popular sense).

What of the special insight into what is right that religion is supposed to provide? Doesn't this give religious people an edge over non-religious people? We may all have similar motivation and similar general moral goals, but doesn't religion provide direct information on the best *means* of reaching these goals?

There are two main difficulties here. The first is that there is disagreement, even among religious people, over whether or not religions give *special* moral guidance, greater than that which may be found through non-religious wisdom traditions and serious ethical inquiry by non-religious people. Accordingly, many people (both religious and non-religious) will simply deny that religions offer direct access to knowledge of right and wrong and hence an inside track on morality. Some individuals and groups still believe this, but the question has by no means been settled.

The second difficulty is that all religions appear to have made serious mistakes in moral matters at points in their history, so that it is necessary to assess their moral prescriptions. This means that the value of special moral revelation, even if it occurs, is limited since whatever is revealed must be independently checked, using precisely the kinds of criteria that reflective non-religious people would use.

But what about the indwelling of the divine spirit? Doesn't the divine order work on people directly to enable them to live morally? Even if at the purely human level, religious people (in the popular sense) have no special access to moral insight and motivation, don't they have supernatural help to live good lives? Perhaps. However, whether or not supernatural phenomena of this kind occur is a matter of controversy. Some people may accept it "on faith," but they must do precisely that: there is at present no adequate factual basis for their belief. Moreover, even if there is divine action of this kind, it doesn't seem to work in favor of religious people, in moral matters at least. On average, non-religious people appear to be just as decent, thoughtful, kind, reliable, and so forth as religious people. There would seem to be no grounds, then, either theoretical or empirical, for dismissing non-religious people as less morally upright. They may not have religious faith in the usual sense; but, on the whole, they have a fair degree of moral goodness.

Religious People Can Be Moral

To say that religious people (in the popular sense) can be moral may appear to be stating the obvious. However, it needs to be said, since it has sometimes been denied by critics of religion. Some maintain that religious people are so taken up with dogmas, rituals, and authoritarian structures that they can't show ordinary human decency in everyday situations. They lose the spirit of the law among the letters. And their "love of God" takes them to a level of metaphysical preoccupation such that the capacity for straightforward love of fellow human beings is lost. The caricatures of the Pharisees in the New Testament and the Puritans in English literature suggest this view of religious people.

Religions, however, are ambiguous and open to differences of interpretation and practice. They can undermine morality, but they can also foster it; and even in a community where religion tends to undermine morality for some people, particular individuals and sub-groups can resist this tendency by understanding and practising the religion differently. Many of the strongest critiques of the moral conduct of religious people come from within religion, thus suggesting that it is not religion as such which subverts morality but rather particular approaches to it. As we observed earlier, religion is an important mediator of morality for many people. Much of their moral formation may be attributed to their religious upbringing, and their morality continues to be supported by religious beliefs, practices, and community ties. The fact that other people who use non-religious mediating structures are equally moral does not detract from the role of religion for religious people.

Many religions are known to have had substantial moral concerns since their early days. With Judaism, the Ten Commandments are largely moral in import. "Right living" in a clearly moral sense of the term was stressed by Siddhartha Gautama as he established his early Buddhist community. Confucianism has always been so morally oriented that some people question its status as a religion (wrongly, I believe). For Jesus, the Golden Rule and several related moral principles were fundamental to the approach to life he envisaged. And Islam was seen by Muhammad as addressing effectively the many moral problems of his day. Indeed, *religions historically have been much more concerned with morality than many of their current adherents realize.* There is often a tendency to "over-spiritualize" religion to the point where serious moral problems affecting the lives of individuals and groups are neglected. Morality is perhaps not the main point of a religion, but it must be a major dimension if the well-being of its members and other people whom it affects are to be adequately provided for.

Because religions have a strong traditional dimension, we often assume that they will hinder "modernization" and moral reform, and hence that religious people will be less moral than non-religious people. However, in our "progress"-oriented age we should constantly remind ourselves of the importance of tradition in maintaining morality. Even in largely non-religious, "modern," urban communities, many of the sustaining concepts, rules, and patterns of life go back hundreds and indeed thousands of years. In this respect, religious communities differ from non-religious ones only in the extent to which aspects of their way of life are codified, labelled, and formally taught. Long tradition is present in each case. Further, in both religious and non-religious communities tradition can play a crucial role in moral reform. "Return to the traditions" is a constant theme of proponents (as well as opponents) of reform.

Both religious and non-religious communities can and must practise what Huston Smith has aptly called "deliberate tradition." This, according to Smith, was Confucius's ingenious answer to the central social problem of his day, namely, how to "preserve true continuity with the past" while taking "sufficient account of new factors that now render the old answers inapplicable." He says:

> Confucius's answer met both requirements superbly. Continuity was preserved by keeping the tradition in the center of the picture. . . . And yet it wasn't the old answer. All the way through Confucius was reinterpreting, modifying. . . .
>
> The shift from spontaneous to deliberate tradition requires that the powers of critical intelligence be turned both to continuing the force of tradition

> intact and to determining what ends tradition shall henceforth serve.[4]

If we adopt this approach, as I believe we should, there is no reason why religious tradition should stand in the way of morality. Or, putting the point more positively, if we are willing to introduce necessary changes over time, religious tradition can play a major role in enabling religious people to be moral.

The Problem of Moral Diversity

I have been arguing that, on the whole, religious and non-religious people are as moral and immoral as each other. Morally, there is no "one true way," no path which by its fruits is seen to be superior to all others. Nor, usually, are there "evil" paths, ones which in general lead to a lower level of morality.

But if this is so, how are we to explain the diversity in moral beliefs and practices around the world and over time? Is polygamy just as good as monogamy? Is head-hunting an acceptable practice? Is there nothing wrong with infanticide? Is a religious regime which forbids the drinking of alcohol no better than one which does not? If there is nothing to choose between one form of behavior and another, doesn't this mean that morality is purely relative, just a matter of what is accepted in a particular culture?

In response to these concerns, the first point to make is that some moral beliefs and practices are indeed better than others, but no one path — religious or non-religious — is without moral shortcomings. The society of ancient Greece may have practised slavery; but the Christianity of nineteenth-century England, for its part, went along with

4. H. Smith, *The Religions of Man* (New York: Harper and Row, Perennial Library, 1965), pp. 176-77.

cruel exploitation of workers. Some "primitive" religions have indeed condoned head-hunting; but many of the "great" religions have celebrated war and imperialism. Some societies have accepted unsatisfactory forms of polygamy; but others have imposed oppressive forms of monogamous marriage. Every religion and culture has skeletons in its closet. And there is not conclusive evidence that any one path or religion consistently has less than others.

Often the same immoralities take different forms in different societies. The sexism of one society which prohibits women from mixing with men physically may be matched by the sexism of another society which keeps women and men culturally apart, despite the appearance of mixing. The formal caste system of one society may, in another society, find its counterpart in informal but equally degrading differences of status and wealth. One society, then, may appear more immoral than another in a particular area without actually being different in practice.

Again, as we saw in Chapter 2, two different societies often pursue the same ends by means of different practices. In these cases, one set of practices is not more moral than the other: it is simply different. Monogamy is used in some societies to try to ensure that a basic level of justice is attained in marriage; whereas other societies allow polygamy but strive to protect the rights of the parties through general marriage laws and practices. Some societies maintain social stability largely through a rigid family structure with strict rules of obedience to elders; while other societies place more emphasis on respect for public authority figures and the political and legal system.

The moral differences between religions and cultures should not be accepted uncritically: we should not fall into cultural relativism. As we saw in Chapter 2, it is possible to make major mistakes in moral matters, and this applies to cultures as well as individuals. However, the work of ethical criticism and reform should chiefly be directed toward *particular* immoral beliefs and practices. There is at present no reason to expect we will find religious or "non-religious" systems which are *in general* inferior from an ethical point of view.

At this point, there may be a flood of objections from people who feel very strongly (and rightly so) about particular issues. Feminists may argue that those societies which are more clearly sexist in their beliefs and practices are obviously inferior. People especially involved in the fight against racism may judge a religion such as that of the Afrikaaners in South Africa to be entirely unacceptable. Environmentalists may regard a religion such as Christianity, which has encouraged its people to go out and "subdue the earth" and accepted industrialization, modern warfare, and the nuclear arms build-up, as simply not in the same league as Hinduism and Buddhism. And one could go on. But these arguments, taken together, tend to support rather than undermine the position that all religions and cultures have had and still have major moral weaknesses, and none is to be identified as in general superior. Instead of rejecting a tradition outright, a better course usually is to work for its reform (whether as an insider or an outsider), trying to increase the extent to which it provides support for sound morality and general well-being.

CHAPTER 5

Whose Well-Being?

Values are meant to promote well-being. But a question which arises repeatedly in ethics and everyday life is: *Whose* well-being? In seeking the good life we can do so purely selfishly; or by favoring one group over others; or by treating everyone equally; or by sacrificing ourselves for others. Which is the appropriate emphasis? Should our pursuit of life goals be individual or communal, egoistic or altruistic?

Self or Others?

My basic answer to this question is that we should seek *both* our own well-being *and* the well-being of others. We should resist pressures to go to one of the extremes: to live only for ourselves or only for others.

The reasons for seeking the well-being of others are many. In the first place, concern for others comes naturally to human beings: helping others is one of the basic values noted in Chapter 2. Except in unusual circumstances, humans want others — especially close relatives, friends, and fellow community members, but also complete strangers — to be happy and are upset when they suffer misfortune.

Altruism is also justifiable in terms of "enlightened self-interest." By helping others we frequently help ourselves. Most obviously, if we do things for others they will often do things for us. The idea "I'll scratch your back if you scratch mine" has a place. While it should not be our sole reason for helping others, it is a basic understanding in most enduring relationships, including close friendships. Another reason for helping others is that the well-being of those around us is often inseparable from our own. If our family and friends prosper, we tend to share their prosperity. At a more general level, our well-being is linked to that of the larger community and society. If the society in which we live is flourishing and free of undue tension and violence, this will typically improve our own quality of life.

Helping others, then, is not just an arbitrary moral requirement; humans have *reason* to be altruistic. Socrates claimed that when people fail to be altruistic, it is because they do not grasp this insight: they do not have a vision of the "full good life" lived in a household and community which meets our most basic needs. While this is not the whole story, since we sometimes have a vision but are unable to live up to it, nevertheless lack of awareness of the advantages of mutually caring relationships is a key explanation of selfish behavior.

While helping others is justified, however, so is the direct pursuit of our own well-being. There are several reasons for this. First, we have special insight into our own needs, and this calls for a "division of labor" in meeting them. Because we know our own nature and circumstances intimately, we are often best able to promote our well-being. A system in which everyone looked after other people's needs and not their own would be extremely inefficient. Second, the desire for our own well-being is very strong. Even people who claim to "live only for others," if observed closely, may be seen to pay considerable attention to their own welfare. This natural interest, far from being suppressed, should be put to work: it gives motivation for steady application to pursuing values. And third, if we literally gave no attention to our own welfare, we would soon become so impoverished physically, mentally, and socially that we wouldn't be able to help others.

But what of the case where it is either my life (or job or friendship) or that of someone else? I can save another person from drowning, for example, only at the expense of my own life. How in such an instance can the principle of pursuing both my well-being and that of others be preserved?

To begin with, it is not a foregone conclusion what would be right in such a situation. Perhaps I should sacrifice myself; but I might not do so and still be a moral person. There are strong reasons, both self-interested and altruistic, on both sides. People who use such examples in arguing for extreme altruism assume that it is obvious what we should do, namely, sacrifice ourselves; but it is not. This kind of dilemma simply strengthens the argument for a balanced position, since we are indeed faced with a dilemma and not a foregone conclusion. The other point to note is that pure "either/or" cases are quite rare. We shouldn't see them as usual, and conclude that it is always necessary to go to one extreme or the other. In most instances a third alternative is available, one which serves both our own well-being and that of others.

But is it psychologically possible to have a balanced concern for self and others? Some claim that all our actions are self-interested: we help others because we want to, which means we hope to gain satisfaction from it. However, as noted earlier, humans to a degree have direct sympathy for others. We often do things for other people knowing full well that it won't maximize our own happiness. Even if we get *some* satisfaction from helping others, this doesn't mean that we do it solely for that reason. A major additional reason may simply be our concern for them.

In concluding this section, we might note that the word "selfishness" applies not to all self-concern, but rather to *undue* self-centredness. As we have seen, considerable interest in our own welfare is essential for any viable — and moral — way of life. While we should reject "selfishness," then, we can nevertheless embrace a balanced concern for both self and others.

A Group Orientation

Just as it is necessary to attend to our own individual needs, so we must give special attention to the groups to which we belong. These include, for example, our "inner group" of family and close friends, the neighborhood community in the area where we live, and perhaps the members of a religious, cultural, or ethnic sub-group.

The reasons for a group orientation in some ways parallel those for self-concern outlined in the previous section. They include the following:

- We have special knowledge of the needs of our groups, and this calls for a division of labor in meeting them: we are in a good position to promote their welfare.
- Most people have a relatively strong desire to help the members of the groups to which they belong, and this motivation, rather than being suppressed, should be put to work in promoting the well-being of these groups.
- In turn, the members of the groups to which we belong are aware of our needs, and we should build up a relationship of understanding and mutual help with them since they can help us so effectively in times of need.
- If we consistently neglect the needs of people who are close to us, this will tend to have a hardening effect on

us, even if we are doing so because of some "high" ideal or cause.

• Unless we have a rich life and strong support at a group level, we may become so impoverished culturally and spiritually that we will be unable to be of much help to people further afield.

The importance of friendship and other personal relationships was recognized by classical Greek philosophers. Aristotle, for example, saw friendship as a *virtue* and emphasized the need for special attachment to a relatively small community, the *polis,* without which (as Socrates had said) life would not be worth living.

Recently, the issue of friendship, family, and relationships of sharing and care has been raised by a number of writers. Lawrence Blum in *Friendship, Altruism, and Morality* claims that the moral life must have an affective dimension, involving compassion, sympathy, and a direct concern for other people's well-being. He questions Kant's emphasis on impartiality and his exclusion of emotion from moral motivation. Blum says that "our emotions and feelings can reflect on us morally," and that "a friendship which involves a very deep and genuine regard for the friend's good is a morally excellent relationship."[1] Carol Gilligan in *In a Different Voice* argues that a relationships and care orientation in ethics is at least as moral as the individualistic, justice orientation which in modern times has been considered morally superior. She documents the damage done to individuals and groups by the neglect and indeed suppression of an ethic of relationships and care.[2] Debra Shogan in *Care and Moral Motivation* states that "proximity to another in a family makes it possible

1. L. Blum, *Friendship, Altruism, and Morality* (London: Routledge and Kegan Paul, 1980), pp. 4-7, 68, 169.
2. C. Gilligan, *In a Different Voice* (Cambridge, MA: Harvard University Press, 1982), *passim.*

to be aware of another's problems as well as how this person might flourish," and further that "physical proximity to others can make it easier to respond to others because we are able to see them as particular individuals rather than as members of humanity . . . ."[3]

As with self-concern, attention to the needs of our inner group or local community should not be unduly at the expense of other people. We should recognize that all humans have as much *right* to well-being as the members of our groups, and we should do a considerable amount to further their welfare. We should not rationalize our group orientation using notions of religious, racial, ethnic, or cultural superiority. And we should press for ingenious social, political, and economic solutions to national and global problems which will provide both for our groups and for the other members of the human family.

It should be noted that an inner group or sub-group orientation is not normally appropriate when we turn to broader political, legal, and administrative responsibilities. Obviously, heads of state, judges, school principals, and police officers, in their respective official capacities, are not usually entitled to favor their own personal groups (although they may correct injustices toward their own groups, as part of an affirmative action program). They are appointed and paid to look after a much wider population. However, in their private lives such people should not neglect their family, friendships, and other relationships; otherwise they may seriously undermine both their personal well-being and their effectiveness in their official roles.

3. D. Shogan, *Care and Moral Motivation* (Toronto: OISE Press, 1988), p. 73.

Society and the Individual

Going beyond inner groups and sub-groups, we turn to the broader societal perspective. As noted in Chapter 2, only individuals — not societies — can experience well-being. However, it is a mistake to conclude that therefore society is of little or no importance. Building up the "health" of a society is a crucial means to promoting the welfare of its members. Many of the problems of individual people today are "structural" or "systemic": they are due largely to weaknesses in society, over which individuals by themselves have little control.

Life in the modern West has become excessively individualistic in many ways. Emphasis on individual effort, fulfilment, and identity is important; but there is need for a parallel emphasis on communal identity and loyalty. There have been times when people have been willing to live and indeed die for their society, because of their sense of identification with it, and we have admired them as human beings. We must not too easily give up the general notion and spirit of membership in a society.

A broad societal perspective is justified partly because, as noted earlier, we are naturally concerned about the welfare of people beyond our own circle. But even from a self-interested point of view the larger society is of crucial significance. It provides much of the infrastructure for our personal and sub-group life. Its atmosphere and ethos constantly affect our quality of life, no matter how much we try to shield ourselves from its influence. It gives us a realm of greater freedom and anonymity when things go wrong at a small group level. And it may be all we have to fall back on if our sub-groups disappear.

Problems which show poor "health" in society include: racial, religious, and ethnic prejudice and conflict, class and sex bias, an unduly materialistic outlook, widespread violence, lack of political interest and understanding, lack of originality and diversity of thought and culture, enthusiasm for inappropriate and excessively costly technology, and pollution of the environment. These need to be tackled directly, as *societal* problems. Admittedly they are also individual problems which should be dealt with at an individual level, notably through education. But they are societal in that they are inherent in the laws, authority relationships, and economic arrangements and practices of society, and largely determine how individuals *must* live if they aren't to become social outcasts.

Adopting a societal perspective means that the wishes of individuals and sub-groups are often overruled by the larger society. This presents certain risks: in the past, appeal to "the greater good" has frequently been used to justify abuse by an élite. However, some curtailment of individual and sub-group demands is essential both to achieve greater equality in society and to promote the health of society in ways which will ultimately benefit everyone. It is ironic that "democracy," which means rule by the people, has so widely come to be understood as "every man for himself," such that there is minimal group direction in key areas of social life.

While increased emphasis on societal matters is needed today, however, we must be wary of going too far (or inappropriately) in this direction. Some "communitarian" writers are inclined to make absolutes out of societal values, losing sight of individual well-being as the ultimate goal. For example, Roberto Unger in *Knowledge and Politics* says that we must "take the ends which men share in their groups as the indicators of the right or good,"[4] and Robert Paul Wolff in *The Poverty of Liberalism* states that "the free society is good as an end in itself for *it is itself a social value*!"[5] Unger and Wolff also place too

4. R. Unger, *Knowledge and Politics* (New York: The Free Press, 1979), p. 103.
5. R. P. Wolff, *The Poverty of Liberalism* (Boston: Beacon Press, 1968), p. 193. His italics and exclamation mark.

much emphasis on "shared" values (important though they are), playing down the extent to which individual needs differ and conflict. Unger says that "community is held together by an allegiance to common purposes"[6] and that there is "a unitary human nature (which) constitutes the final basis of moral judgment" (p. 221). And Wolff speaks of "pluralism" as a theory which "played a valuable role during one stage in America's development and which has now lost its value either as description or prescription."[7] While it once met a need, now "new problems confront America, problems not of distributive justice but of the common good . . . . We must give up the image of society as a battleground of competing groups" (p. 161).

Clearly, the insights of communitarians and individualists must be combined. We should acknowledge the crucial importance of societal structures, but also see them as means to the ultimate end of individual well-being. And we should recognize the extent to which humans are alike and need to develop shared values, but also accept diversity and pluralism.

A Global Orientation

Today our concern for well-being must extend beyond particular societies to the global community. This doesn't mean that the individual, the group, or the society should be neglected. Individual well-being is still the ultimate goal; and groups and societies are essential mediating structures. But social and economic theory must be rewritten to include the largely ignored global context. With worldwide communications, global cultural, political, and economic influences, and an endangered earth ecosystem,

6. *Knowledge and Politics*, p. 220.
7. *The Poverty of Liberalism*, p. 123.

we live in a radically new world. As Graham Pike and David Selby have observed:

> Global interdependencies . . . affect the purity of the air we breathe and the water we drink; the levels of employment and inflation; the price of tea; the level of taxation; fuel costs; the survival prospects of wildlife; the availability and subject matter of the books and newspapers we read; the changing roles of men and women in society; our relative peacefulness or unpeacefulness of mind and our image of the future.[8]

The reasons for promoting global well-being are similar to ones noted earlier. On the one hand, we have a natural concern for all human beings, including those in far off countries whose needs and sufferings are brought to our attention daily by the media. On the other hand, our well-being and that of our "inner group" and society is bound up with the welfare of the human race as a whole and the health of the planet. Just as we cannot escape the influence of our society, so today we are affected by happenings in every part of the globe.

In the past, it was often easy to dismiss the needs of people in foreign countries — if we heard about them — on the ground that they were vastly different from us, "primitives" or "pagans" or even evil people who deserved their misfortunes. But as our knowledge of other cultures and peoples grows, this attitude is difficult to sustain or justify. Robin Richardson has written about the way in which our negative images of other people are often dispelled by greater knowledge. He describes how a character in a novel by Thomas Hardy changed his conception of farm-folk as "country bumpkins," "yokels,"

8. G. Pike and D. Selby, "Global Education," in *Controversial Issues in Curriculum*, ed. J. Wellington (Oxford: Blackwell, 1986), p. 40.

"peasants." After just a few days' residence in the country, his stereotype "had been disintegrated into a number of varied fellow-creatures — beings of many minds, beings infinite in difference; some happy, many serene, a few depressed, one here and there bright even to genius, some stupid, others wanton, others austere . . . ." Richardson goes on to apply the point to people of other lands. He says that in the autumn of 1979, "when most of the Western media were frantic with indignation against Iran," one journalist wrote as follows:

> Iranians are not all students, mullahs or heroin smugglers. There are Iranian plumbers, birdwatchers, piano-tuners, potters, horticulturalists, weavers, and hairdressers. There are lazy, timid, depressed Iranians, Iranians who hate crowds, agoraphobic and claustrophobic Iranians, and Iranians who bite their nails. Some Iranians dislike the East as much as others dislike the West. Some believe in women's equality and abhor violence of any kind. Some are even atheist . . . .[9]

Richardson's basic message is that people in other parts of the world — even those we might regard as "enemies" at a particular time — are varied, purposeful human beings like ourselves, just as worthy of understanding, acceptance, and well-being.

A global perspective is necessitated by scarcity in the world. This was pointed out in the late sixties by Garrett Hardin in his classic paper "The Tragedy of the Commons."[10] He compares the world ecosystem to a medieval village commons which all use to graze their herds.

9. R. Richardson, in D. Hicks and C. Townley, *Teaching World Studies* (London: Longman, 1982), pp. 24-25.
10. G. Hardin, "The Tragedy of the Commons," *Science* (1968), **162**, 1243-48.

The various nations of the world — notably the minority of nations which consume the majority of resources — have shortsightedly pursued their separate interests. They have failed to realize that there are limits to the resources that the world commons can provide and have thought only of the proportion they can win for themselves. Paul Ehrlich and Richard Harriman, building on Hardin's analysis, say:

> . . . the only hope for dealing with the problem of the commons is "mutual coercion, mutually agreed upon." One should not be instantly repelled by the term coercion. Appeals for the voluntary exercise of restraint in relation to the commons have proven notoriously ineffective. We do not pay our taxes on the honor system . . . . Hardin argues that an appeal to responsibility puts an individual in a hopeless double bind. On one hand, it produces fear of societal disapproval if he does not behave in the proper way towards the commons. On the other hand, it produces the fear that if he restrains himself others will take advantage and exploit the commons more. . . .
>
> . . . A first step, of course, is the creation of a climate of opinion within nations which favors some relinquishment of sovereignty of national governments. . . . All nations must come to view nonrenewable resources as being held in trust for all mankind, present and future. And all mankind must have a say in their use.[11]

But scarcity is not the only problem. Much of the harm done to other peoples in the world today is due to the

11. P. Ehrlich and R. Harriman, *How to Be a Survivor: A Plan to Save Spaceship Earth* (New York: Ballantine Books, 1971), pp. 114-16.

gratuitous imposition on them ("for their own good") of patterns of life which don't suit them, which they cannot afford, and which are not working well even in the societies of origin. Some of this cultural imperialism is motivated by acquisitiveness, by the desire to create new markets and hence gain a greater share of the world's goods. But much of it is due to unfounded smugness about our way of life, and lack of regard for the traditions and ongoing wisdom of other peoples.

The Goal of Equality

The ideal community — locally, nationally, globally — is one in which there is equality of well-being. To the question "Whose well-being?" an appropriate answer is "Everyone's, equally." However, the justification of this principle is complex and its implementation is difficult. Here we can only touch on some aspects of the issue.

The first point to note is that what is in question is equality of *well-being*. Different people may achieve equal well-being in different ways, and so may not be equal in all respects. For example, some people place special emphasis on travel, others on socializing and entertaining, others on pursuing courses of study, and others on aesthetic experience. If as a result there are inequalities in knowledge of other countries, social skills, artistic attainment, and so on, this is not an inequitable situation in a negative sense. Equality is not of absolute value, to be pursued without regard for the well-being of the people involved.

Under specific conditions, however, inequalities certainly result in inequality of well-being. For example, in modern industrial societies lack of access to education, meaningful employment, and positions of power and status typically (though not always) results in a reduction of well-being. Part of the task of social science and political theory is to find out which inequalities lead to inequalities of well-being under which circumstances.

We should recognize that inequality affects less privileged people in at least two ways. Not only are they denied basic goods — food, shelter, health, leisure, status, and so on — important for well-being, but also they suffer from a sense of indignity and injustice because of their unequal position. As Alan Brown says, paraphrasing John Rawls:

> . . . the worse-off have to be compensated for the introduction of . . . inequality because that inequality will undermine at least one important social primary good — self-respect. This is not because of envy. It is simply because those that do less well will feel inferior.[12]

In the past, especially in isolated regions, this sense of indignity could partly be overcome by ideologies which rationalized inequality. Today, however, as debates about social justice along with soap operas about the rich and famous are beamed even to remote parts of the Third World, this secondary result of inequality is difficult to avoid. This is one reason why it is no longer feasible to return to earlier social arrangements — as advocated by some communitarians — where there was great inequality but the poor knew their place and (we are told) found meaning in it.

Equality (of well-being) is justifiable on the dual grounds noted before in this chapter: concern for others and enlightened self-interest. The first "argument" involves simply an appeal to our basic desire for the well-being of other humans — locally, societally, and globally

12. A. Brown, *Modern Political Philosophy: Theories of the Just Society* (Harmondsworth: Penguin, 1986), p. 60.

— with the assumption that all humans are equally deserving of well-being.

The argument from enlightened self-interest is more complex. The basic insight is that *inequality has harmful consequences for the privileged person which counter the advantages of privilege.* This has been noted with respect to the family, where imbalances of power and privilege can greatly undermine relationships between husband and wife, and also between parents and children, to the detriment of *both* parties in each case. While husbands, for example, are typically privileged in today's world, the benefits and satisfaction they gain from their marriage are often considerably less than would be the case in an equal relationship. Of course, for many men (and perhaps women) the capacity to live in an equal relationship is a new skill which would have to be learned; but the argument from self-interest assumes that with time it could be attained, at least to a degree.

Paulo Freire, discussing relations between the rich and the poor in South America (and beyond), makes a similar point at the societal level. He claims that the rich are themselves harmed by their role as oppressors. For example, they accept and live by the alienating, materialistic, competitive ideologies they employ in keeping the poor in their place. They lose the capacity to be "more fully human": they experience a dehumanization "which marks not only those whose humanity has been stolen, but also (though in a different way) those who have stolen it . . . ." The oppressors themselves stand in need of liberation so that they may live full, human lives.[13]

According to Alan Brown, "there are two ways in which . . . privilege might be argued to be bad for those who possess it." The first is that "the rich man is risking

13. P. Freire, *Pedagogy of the Oppressed* (New York: Herder and Herder, 1972), for example, pp. 27-36.

revolution by maintaining his privilege" and so "may be well-advised to make concessions." Brown plays down this argument (a little too much, I believe) on the ground that "history tells us that terror and repression may work just as well (if not better) than concession and conciliation." The second and main argument in Brown's view is along the lines we have been discussing. His statement of it is worth quoting at length:

> . . . everyone has a direct interest in everyone enjoying the basic goods (of life) . . . . That interest will arise because the activities and social relations which comprise the good life so define it. If, for example, the good life involves relationships of trust and friendship and precludes relationships of dominance and coercion, then we have the beginnings of an argument which will show that it is reasonable for everyone to accept our criterion.
>
> The more familiar arguments to this effect focus on the merits of equality (at least of a rough social kind). Thinkers, from Christ to Marx, have argued that the rich as well as the poor suffer from inequality. The central idea for us is that societies characterized by inequalities (at least at that level proscribed by our criterion) are unreasonable because the activities and social relations therein are destructive of the good life for everyone concerned.[14]

We should not underestimate, however, the difficulty of the transition to equality, no matter how reasonable the ideal may be. As Freire has pointed out, it involves a fundamental shift in outlook on the part of privileged and underprivileged people alike. "Liberation is . . . a childbirth, and a painful one." The type of person who

14. *Modern Political Philosophy*, p. 171.

emerges is a new being, "viable only as the oppressor–oppressed contradiction is superseded by the humanization of all . . . ."[15]

David Lane, in his study of Eastern European socialist societies, has documented how social stratification persisted in those communities despite the most sincere and concerted efforts to overcome it. Even where private property was abolished, differential *control* of (state) property continued. According to Lane, so long as different jobs in society have different levels of insight and authority associated with them, differences in income and prestige tend to persist. Lane does not reject social equality as a worthy ideal, but he argues that attainment of it requires much more radical social, economic, and ideational restructuring than has been achieved to date.[16]

But the failure of these socialist regimes to achieve equality certainly does not provide a vindication of the capitalist way. The extreme (and growing) difference between rich and poor in capitalist countries represents a serious problem for all. In our time the United States is an object lesson in the deterioration of the quality of life for *everyone* in an unequal system. And Sweden offers an example of how a nation can do quite well economically while experiencing the social advantages of at least relative equality.

There is a long way to go in finding feasible ways to achieve equality of well-being. However, I hope enough has been said to show that it is a goal worth pursuing much more energetically than we have to date. As with other value areas, identifying the good and seeing its appropriateness is at least half the battle. A major educa-

15. *Pedagogy of the Oppressed*, p. 33.
16. D. Lane, *The End of Inequality? Stratification under State Socialism* (Harmondsworth: Penguin, 1971), especially pp. 129-37.

tional program is needed to help people see (a) that inequality of well-being is neither natural nor necessary; (b) that certain people are not more deserving of privilege by virtue of religion, race, ethnicity, gender, and so forth; and (c) that greater equality, if pursued in feasible ways, can lead to greater well-being even for people who are currently privileged.

Part Two:

Patterns of Values

In Adulthood

An understanding of adult psychological development is important background for discussing adult values learning and education. In Part Two, we will first look at phase and stage theories of development, with special attention to their value aspects. Then I will show, as a corrective to these theories, that there is continuity as well as change in values during adulthood. Finally, as an area of particular interest, we will consider gender differences (and similarities) in adult values.

At times the discussion in this part of the book becomes rather academic, with extensive reference to what other authors have said. Obviously I think this material is important, but readers should feel free to simply skim it, depending on their interests.

CHAPTER 6

Phases of Adult Development: Seasons and Passages

One way of understanding adult values is in terms of life "phases." Adults have somewhat different values and value concerns at different points in "the adult life cycle." According to strict phase theory, these different "seasons" of life are not better or worse than each other: they are just different. At each period of life different needs emerge requiring new strategies, including new (but not better) value solutions.

In this chapter we will look at three phase theories: those of Daniel Levinson, Gail Sheehy, and Erik Erikson. While I believe there is some value in a phase approach to adulthood, I will make two major criticisms of existing phase theories. First, they are unclear, often mixing a phase approach with a "stage" notion (the idea that later phases are better than earlier ones). Second, phase theories often greatly exaggerate the phase shifts of adulthood, and as a result distort and stereotype the values of adults of various age-groups.

I will conclude the chapter by looking at the dangers *and contributions* of a phase approach. Although phase theories have many weaknesses, there are, as I said in the Introduction, insights to be gained from them which can be of great help in living the good life. Paradoxically, we first have to criticize these theories in order to benefit from what they have to offer.

Phases or Stages? A Confused Picture

In *The Seasons of a Man's Life,* Daniel Levinson claims that adults pass through roughly twenty-year "eras" and five-year "periods" in their lives.[1] The Early Adult era includes Early Adult Transition (17–22), Entering the Adult World (22–28), Age 30 Transition (28–33), and Settling Down (33–40). The Middle Adulthood era contains the periods of Mid-Life Transition (40–45), Entering Middle Adulthood (45–50), Age 50 Transition (50–55), and Culmination of Middle Adulthood (55–60). The Late Adulthood era begins with Late Adult Transition (60–65) and continues until the age of eighty, when it is followed by the Late Late Adulthood era (80+).

Levinson states that his is not a stage theory, that is, one which sees each phase as an improvement on those which came before. He says of both Erik Erikson's theory (on which he draws heavily) and his own that they "posit a sequence that is not hierarchical. One period is not higher or better than the preceding ones. . . . Spring is not intrinsically a better season than winter, nor is summer better than spring" (p. 319). The transitions from one period to another may be successful or unsuccessful: "There are losses as well as gains in the shift from every period or era to the next" (p. 320). By contrast, he says,

1. D. Levinson, *The Seasons of a Man's Life* (New York: Ballantine Books, 1978). See especially the chart on page 57.

there are "the stage theories of Lawrence Kohlberg, Jean Piaget and Jane Loevinger" which "describe developmental stages that follow an ascending or hierarchical order: a person advances from one level to the next, each stage representing a higher capability" (p. 319).

However, Levinson is not in fact successful in giving a non-hierarchical account of life phases. He qualifies his claim that later periods are not better or more advanced by adding "except in the general sense that each period builds upon the work of the earlier ones and represents a later phase in the cycle" (p. 320). He doesn't seem to realize that this qualification has crucial implications. If later phases, when successfully negotiated, incorporate the attainments of earlier periods, this inevitably means that well-functioning adults become progressively more complete and capable, psychosocially (and morally) as they grow older.

At a few points this implication of Levinson's position becomes explicit in his own writing. For example, he compares adolescents unfavorably to adults. "The preadult era is a time of extraordinary growth but it is only a prelude to adult living. Its result is an immature and still vulnerable individual making his entry into the adult world" (p. 21). Elsewhere, Levinson includes younger adults among the relatively immature:

> The required work of middle adulthood is different from that of youth. It involves greater responsibilities, perspective, and judgment. A person in this era must be able to care for younger and older adults, to exercise authority creatively, to transcend the youthful extremes of shallow conformity and impulsive rebelliousness. (p. 329)

It is true that Levinson goes on to say that "the moderate mid-life decrease in biological capacity must be counterbalanced by an increased psychosocial capacity." However, in a technologically advanced society, such as ours in the West, the psychosocial advantage described by Levinson would seem to outweigh the "moderate" biological disadvantage, at least in middle age. And even if it does not, the fact remains that Levinson is claiming superiority in psychosocial matters — including values — for older adults. Accordingly, the supposed non-judgmental character of his phase account is lost.

Gail Sheehy in *Passages: Predictable Crises of Adult Life* also advocates a phase theory. She postulates definite age points and periods in adult life which present distinctive challenges or "crises."[2] These include Pulling Up Roots (age 18-22), The Trying Twenties, Catch-30, Rooting and Extending (early 30s), and The Deadline Decade (age 35-45). Referring to the various passages or turning points of life, she says that they appeared "with a relentless regularity at the same ages" for the adults she studied (p. 14).

However, Sheehy goes even further than Levinson in attempting to graft a stage theory onto her phase theory. She speaks of a goal for adult development, namely, the achievement of "autonomy," "self-sufficiency," or "authenticity" (for example, pp. 31, 36, 39, 44, 52-56). The ultimate objective, she says, is to arrive at "that felicitous state of inner expansion in which we know of all our potentialities and possess the ego strength to direct their full reach" (pp. 48-49). This state becomes possible only after we have arrived at "true adulthood" (late thirties to

2. G. Sheehy, *Passages: Predictable Crises of Adult Life* (New York: Bantam, 1977), *passim*. See also her *Pathfinders* (New York: William Morrow and Company, 1981). While Sheehy is not thought of as an academic, the size of her interview group for *Passages* and her inclusion of women in her sample makes the basis of her observations more solid than that of some academics who have written in this area. Also, the detail and sensitivity with which she describes the *possible* crises of adulthood make her writings in many ways more helpful to adult readers, including academics, than other works in the field.

early forties) (p. 49). If we rise to the challenges of this period we may flower into "full authenticity" (p. 49) and enter upon what "may well be the best years" of our life as we pass into later adulthood (p. 46).

Like Levinson, Sheehy is inconsistent in her position. At times she appears to reject the idea of attaching ages to levels of autonomy and authenticity. She says: "Do not take the ages too seriously. The stages are the thing" (p. 37); and: "Human beings, thank God, have an individual inner dynamic that can never be precisely coded" (p. 37). But in fact she ties age periods and developmental stages closely together. She makes constant reference to an "inner" process of unfolding which has its own timetable, its own "developmental rhythms" (p. 22). She refers to the resultant shifts as "changes that are common to our chronological development" (p. 33). Although the people she interviewed could see "no consistency" to the "outer events of their lives" there was "a striking consistency to the inner turmoil they described. At specific points along the life cycle they would feel stirrings . . . . I began to wonder if there were, in fact, turning points in the lives of adults that were *predictable*" (p. 14). Thus, despite her protestations to the contrary, the developmental progress of the well-functioning adult is tied to the crises or turning points to which she assigns such specific ages.

Erik Erikson is usually seen as the classic non-judgmental phase theorist, the one to whom virtually all other phase theorists pay homage. Upon closer examination, however, we find that his is a combination of a phase and a stage theory in much the way that Levinson's and Sheehy's accounts are. Given their acknowledged indebtedness to Erikson, the similarity is not surprising.

Erikson's theory differs from those of Levinson and Sheehy in important ways. For example, he stresses continuities which persist throughout life, saying that each "psychosocial strength" which he has identified "exists in some form before its critical time normally arrives."[3] In an adult we see not only present distinctive characteristics but also "what is left of . . . earlier selves and what is presaged of . . . future ones."[4] Again, Erikson shows awareness of the role of social and cultural factors in adult formation. For example, speaking of the late adulthood phase, Erikson says that the attainment of "integrity" (the distinctive virtue of this period) is possible only with "the firm support of cultural institutions and of the special leader classes representing them."[5] He describes integrity as involving "the most mature faith that an aging person can muster *in his cultural setting and historical period*."[6] Erikson also has a fundamental respect for the importance of young people in a society. He says that "the fashionable insistence on dramatizing the dependence of children on adults often blinds us to the dependence of the older generation on the younger one. . . . Maturity needs guidance as well as encouragement from what has been produced and must be taken care of."[7]

Despite these distinctive insights, however, Erikson's theory shares with Levinson's and Sheehy's the weakness that it combines age-specific phases with developmental stages, while at the same time denying this is what is being done. It claims that well-functioning people in a supportive socio-cultural context become progressively more mature and virtuous as they grow older: that older adults typically attain a level of desirable development which is simply not possible in childhood, adolescence, or earlier adulthood. Erikson outlines eight "ages of man,"

3. E. Erikson, *Childhood and Society*, 2nd ed. (New York: Norton, 1963), p. 271.
4. E. Erikson, *Insight and Responsibility* (New York: Norton, 1964), p. 137.
5. *Childhood and Society*, p. 269.
6. *Ibid.*, p. 272. Italics added.
7. *Ibid.*, pp. 266-67.

each with its distinctive conflict: Basic Trust vs Basic Mistrust; Autonomy vs Shame and Doubt; Initiative vs Guilt; Industry vs Inferiority; Identity vs Role Confusion; Intimacy vs Isolation; Generativity vs Stagnation; Ego Integrity vs Despair. (Of these, the last three are the adult phases.) In each case, the first term in the dyad is the desirable "ego quality" characteristic of the life stage in question. And ideally these qualities are added progressively to one's nature as one grows older: "Each individual, to become a mature adult, must to a sufficient degree develop all the ego qualities mentioned."[8]

Erikson professes to be disappointed that some writers view these positive ego qualities as "an *achievement*, secured once and for all at a given stage," and have even made "an *achievement scale* out of these stages." He comments that this approach represents "a projection on child development of that success ideology which can so dangerously pervade our private and public daydreams," leading us to overlook the "tragic potentials of human life."[9] However, he goes on immediately to outline eight "basic virtues" which emerge at the respective stages and which constitute "a blueprint of essential strengths which evolution has built both into the ground plan of the life stages and into that of man's institutions": namely, hope, will power, purpose, competence, fidelity, love, care, and wisdom.[10] It is difficult to see how one could *avoid* a "success ideology" within a conceptual framework such as this. As we saw with Levinson and Sheehy, the claim that well-functioning individuals pass through a cumulative sequence of increasingly desirable ego stages tied to universal age periods has the inevitable implication that,

8. *Ibid.*, p. 269.
9. *Ibid.*, p. 274.
10. *Ibid.*, p. 274. Erikson gives a more detailed account of these virtues in *Insight and Responsibility*, pp. 111-34.

on average, people become better as they grow older. While tragedies befall older and younger people alike, they do not cancel out the ever-increasing psychosocial superiority and advantage of older people. Levinson, as we have seen, comes closest of the three to providing an effective counter to this implication, suggesting that the advantages and disadvantages of growing older may equal each other. However, he does not develop this idea sufficiently to overcome the general thrust of his position; and Erikson does not have a parallel line of argument at all. Erikson's description of the final "age of man" is positively glowing, depicting a state of integration and balance which one might wish for at an earlier age but which the schedule of unfolding of one's nature renders impossible.[11]

In closing this section, I want to emphasize that I am not here criticizing the stage-improvement assumptions of Levinson, Sheehy, and Erikson. Rather, I am drawing attention to the inconsistencies in their theories and the confusion which results, especially given the theorists' own lack of clarity about what they are doing. In Chapter 7, however, I will argue that stage-improvement notions are themselves mistaken, thus adding to the weaknesses of theories which combine phases and stages.

11. Erikson's most recent book, *Vital Involvement in Old Age* (New York: Norton, 1986), written jointly with his wife, is perhaps more realistic about some of the problems of late adulthood; but I feel it leaves his general position intact. In a joint interview with *The New York Times*, 14 June 1988, when the Eriksons were both in their late eighties, Joan Erikson said: "Lots of old people don't get wise, but you don't get wise unless you age."

The Implausibility of Existing Phase Theories

Apart from confusions and questionable assumptions about improvement with age, the main problem with most phase theories (and again we will concentrate on those of Levinson, Sheehy, and Erikson) is that they exaggerate the extent to which similar things happen in the lives of all adults at the same ages. They make generalizations which from the point of view of ordinary observation seem absurd. While phase theorists claim to have based their conclusions on research, it is clear that something has gone wrong.

Levinson, for example, states that all men experience roughly five-year "periods" in their lives; they begin and end the same periods at virtually the same age; and the periods alternate strictly between transitional phases — Early Adult Transition (17–22), Age Thirty Transition (28–33), and so on — and stable phases — Entering the Adult World (22–28), Settling Down (33–40), and so on (p. 57).

Now, it seems extremely unlikely, from what we see in everyday life, that there are in fact universal five-year male phases, with so *many* of the same things happening to different men at the same ages. Insofar as we can generalize at all, some men change more quickly than others; and in different areas of life, men change at varying rates. Some first experience serious qualms about aging at thirty, others at forty, and others at fifty. Some come to accept major limits on what they can achieve in life in their twenties and others not until their fifties or sixties, with others spread in between.

Further, the claim that these phases alternate neatly between change and stability is undoubtedly mistaken. Surely, at each point in their lives men (and women) are changing in some respects and stable in others. Insofar as change exceeds stability, or vice versa, this may be so for a week, a year, or ten years; and two or four years of *relative* stability may be followed by six or eight years of *relative* instability, or vice versa. And one would expect enormous differences from one person to another in the time and duration of periods of stability, instability, and rough balance of the two.

Interestingly, Levinson acknowledges many of these exceptions to his strict phase demarcations. He says, for example, that his subjects "differed widely in their relationships with parents during the novice phase" (p. 74); that while age seventeen to twenty-two is typically a crisis period, men are "likely to experience at least a moderate crisis . . . somewhere between the late teens and the late twenties" (p. 81); that during the Age Thirty Transition (28–33) "a man has a sense of greater urgency" (p. 85), but also during the Settling Down period (33–40) "a man has a stronger sense of urgency" (p. 139); that the Mid-life Transition (40–45) is a time of "de-illusionment," but "illusion continues to have its place . . . all through the life cycle" (p. 193); that "in every era, a man normally has the need and the capability to generate a legacy" (p. 221); that at age forty a man has "a distinct sense of bodily decline" (p. 22) and "at around 60, there is again the reality and the experience of bodily decline" (p. 34); that "some men make satisfactory provisional choices (of a new life structure) during the Mid-life Transition" but "in most cases, a man . . . may need most of the period of Entering Middle Adulthood to establish the choices on which a new life structure is built" (pp. 278-79); that in the age forty-five to fifty period "many new steps must be taken, and their exact nature and phasing vary widely," and during this period "an integrated structure may emerge early or late . . . or not at all" (p. 279). Despite these many qualifications, however, Levinson continues to assume that there are dramatic phase shifts at universal age points: "one of our greatest surprises," he says, "was the relatively low variability in the age at which every period begins and ends" (p. 318).

Sheehy's claim that there are universal age phases (in her case for women as well as men) is implausible for the same reason that Levinson's is: it simply doesn't square with everyday experience and observation. And Sheehy goes even further than Levinson in providing ammunition against her own theory, giving numerous examples of how in fact adults vary in both the nature and timing of their crises and changes. While this makes her work in some ways more useful than Levinson's, it points up more clearly the problematic nature of her generalizations.

One major type of difference documented by Sheehy is that between women and men. While we will review this material more fully in a later chapter, we might note here such phenomena as (according to Sheehy) fundamentally different reasons for marrying and staying married during the Trying Twenties; and the tendency during the Deadline Decade (35–45) of many women to want to branch out and of many men to wish to consolidate. In the face of observations such as these, how can one say that all people — women as well as men — go through the same phases at the same ages?

Sheehy also describes very different life patterns *within* each gender. Among men there are, for example, Transients (who make no firm commitments in their twenties), Locked Ins (who make perhaps overly solid commitments), and, much less commonly, Integrators (who try to balance family, career, and societal roles) (pp. 253-54). Among women there are Caregivers (who, initially at least, have no aspirations beyond their domestic role), Nurturers Who Defer Achievement, Achievers Who Defer Nurturing, and Integrators (who try to combine marriage, career, and motherhood). The descriptions given of these various types of people suggest basic differences such that they cannot all fit the phase categories outlined by Sheehy.

It may seem strange that Levinson and Sheehy would so extensively document differences in human life patterns and yet continue to insist that there are universal life phases across a wide range of human characteristics and experiences. However, they both have a belief that, in some mysterious way, the individual differences don't detract from the "underlying patterns."

To achieve this magic, Levinson employs the concept of "life structure," defined as "the underlying pattern or design of a person's life" (p. 41). At one point he concedes that in specific aspects of development such as aging, psychological maturity, and career, there is "considerable variability in the ages at which particular changes occur." Further, "specific events such as marriage, starting a family, death of loved ones, and retirement may occur at very different ages." But he goes on to say that "when we look at development in terms of the evolution of *life structure* . . . the periods follow an age-linked sequence" (p. 318). Elsewhere he says: "Individuals go through the periods in infinitely varied ways, but the periods themselves are universal" (p. 322). It is extremely difficult to see how this can be, however, since it is precisely in terms of specific aspects that Levinson has defined the eras and periods and, presumably, assessed the data from his interviewees. The concept of a "life structure" is never independently elucidated.

Sheehy works her magic by means of the concept of "inner unfolding." She says that one should not attach much developmental significance to "marker events" — "the concrete happenings of our lives" such as "graduations, marriage, childbirth, divorce, getting or losing a job." What she is primarily interested in are the "changes that begin within." "The underlying impulse toward change," she says, "will be there regardless of whether or not it is manifested in or accentuated by a marker event" (p. 29). There is, she maintains, a basic personality "unfolding in a sequence of growth" (p. 15) and "always in its essence developing" (pp. 17-18) which can be seen despite the diversity in externals.

But there are two problems here. In the first place, Sheehy says very little about this inner development except that it is toward autonomy, integrity, and the like. Most of her description of the phases is in terms of life events and experiences. If she declares these irrelevant her phases largely evaporate. And secondly, by emphasizing inner development as the central phenomenon of phase changes, Sheehy runs up against the wealth of empirical evidence produced by stage developmentalists. According to Lawrence Kohlberg and a host of other researchers, there is great variability in the age at which particular stages of development are attained, *especially* in adulthood. Thus, whichever tack Sheehy takes, whether toward life experiences (which, she admits, vary considerably from person to person) or toward inner development (which, according to developmentalists, different people achieve at very different ages), her age-linked phase theory appears implausible.

Turning finally — and briefly — to Erikson's position, we find not surprisingly that it too is difficult to defend in light of common human experience. On the face of it, his theory might seem more plausible since it doesn't make such detailed claims about what happens in people's lives at specific ages. As we noted earlier, he only mentions three adult phases — roughly, early, middle, and late adulthood — and it would be reasonable to expect some broad shifts over the sixty years or so which they span. However, while lengthening the phases solves some problems, it creates others. It is highly implausible to suggest that for a full twenty-year period *all* human beings are centrally preoccupied with the problem of intimacy versus isolation (early adulthood), or integrity versus despair (late adulthood); or that a problem with which one has grappled for twenty years in an earlier life phase does not crop up again in major ways during a later twenty-year period. The central difficulty of phase theories, as we will note in the next section, is that they stereotype people; and in some ways this stereotyping is more unbelievable — and outrageous — when applied to a large age group (for example, all forty to sixty year olds) than when it occurs with reference to a smaller age group (for example, all twenty-eight to thirty-three year olds) who might be expected to have more in common.

The Dangers and Contributions of Phase Theories

Phase theories present several dangers which most theorists to date have not guarded against sufficiently. One problem we have already noted and will discuss at length in Chapter 7 arises when phases are also assumed to be stages of *improvement*. This is not a necessary feature of phase theories but it is certainly very common. The central difficulty here is that if younger adults are seen as typically less psychologically (and morally) mature, they will tend to be discriminated against, their views will not be taken as seriously as they should in decision-making, and the quality of relationships between the generations will be considerably lower than it could be, to the detriment of all parties.

Most of the other dangers of phase theories come under the general heading of stereotyping or over-generalization. Phase accounts of adult life have very often resulted in all or most people in a particular age group being seen as having the same problems and characteristics. This once again is not a necessary feature of phase theories since one can build in qualifications which make it clear that there are a great many variations and exceptions; but too frequently this has not been done.

To some extent, theorists such as Erikson, with his glowing account of integrity in late adulthood, and Levinson, with his deliberate move to include "late late adulthood" (80+) in the adult life cycle, have used phase theory to help overcome age-stereotyping. However, they have also often reinforced old stereotypes and created new ones. As we saw earlier, Erikson characterizes all age groups apart from older adults as relatively deficient in one or more basic human virtues. And Levinson projects a strong sense of the psychosocial immaturity of younger adults and the biological decline of older adults. Sheehy for her part moves back and forth between stressing age-similarities and noting individual differences, but she nevertheless maintains that true maturity is only possible after mid-life, and that one is certain to experience severe problems and exhibit considerable immaturity at specific points prior to negotiating that passage.

Another form of stereotyping that has been typical of phase theories is to suggest that a particular change or set of changes is *all* that is of interest at a given age. For example, Erikson's theory can easily lead one to the conclusion that role identity, intimacy, and integrity are not important issues in the lives of the middle adulthood group, whose preoccupation is with generativity; and that well-functioning older adults, striving for integrity, are not confronting new and severe crises of identity and intimacy. Similarly, Sheehy's account of people in their twenties boldly striking out in new directions encourages one to overlook their need to have a sense of meaning in life, to be accepted at certain levels of society, and to confront their mortality. Even if the preoccupation used to define an age-group *is* especially characteristic of that age-group, it is by no means the only significant feature of the group in question. If we overlook this fact, we may approach the age-group in an entirely inappropriate fashion, whether in our personal lives or in educational, social, and political contexts.

Finally, phase theories have tended to represent typical characteristics of age-groups as *inevitable* characteristics, thus leading to a fatalism with respect to the problems and development of adults. For example, just because fifteen years ago it was common for people to have a severe mid-thirties or mid-forties crisis associated with heightened awareness of human limitations and mortality, this doesn't mean that it must happen to a particular individual today. As a result of the increasing reach of the mass media, the changing content of books, magazines, and educational programs, and the spread of world views which adopt a more accepting and matter-of-fact approach to limitation and death, people reaching the mid-thirties and mid-forties today may often not be affected in the same way. And even if many still are, a particular individual can choose to work on these issues earlier in life and either have such crises earlier or perhaps avoid them altogether, at least in a severe form.

Despite their dangers, however, we must not overlook the contributions of phase theories. To begin with, as we will discuss at greater length in Chapter 8, there *are* some phases during adulthood. For example, virtually all human beings experience *gradual* changes over time in strength, agility, and bodily appearance, and in frequency of health problems; and our priorities change somewhat over the years, as we move from creating a way of life to consolidating and integrating elements already established. There are also phases which, though not universal, are widespread in a particular culture: for example, in wealthy industrial societies today, marriage and child rearing are common in the twenties and thirties age-group and retirement from paid work is common among people in their sixties.

Furthermore, being aware of *possible* or *likely* phase changes can certainly be of great value to individuals, groups, and institutions. For example, young adults in Western societies who realize that, in their thirties, they *may* experience a period of extreme anxiety in contemplating their mortality, as described by Sheehy at the beginning of *Passages*, can pursue various avenues to help prepare for and cope with such a development. It need not come as a sudden, devastating surprise as it did to Sheehy. Of course, there are dangers in early awareness of likely future problems in that it may detract from our present happiness. However, there are many ways in which we can prepare for the future without spoiling the present; and besides, vague misgivings about an unknown future can be just as disturbing as a clear grasp of likely future challenges.

As well as helping us prepare for the future, knowledge of phases can enable us to deal better with changes when they occur. This is partly because we have the consolation of knowing that *many* other people experience the same problems, and partly because we have a better grasp of just what is happening. In Sheehy's own case of mid-thirties anxiety, she eventually was able to see that her condition was the result of a multiplicity of factors, each of which had to be dealt with in its own way. She, however, had to identify these elements by herself, while in extreme distress, and without awareness of the "naturalness" of her symptoms given her state of mind and life situation.

At an institutional level, knowledge of *typical* phases can also be an advantage. In education, for example, programs can be developed which help prepare people for the *possibility* of crises in early married life, mid-life career doldrums, difficulties associated with retirement, and so on. In social services, the *possible* needs of unemployed young adults or retired older adults can be assessed with greater accuracy and steps taken to meet them. Levinson toward the end of *The Seasons of a Man's Life* draws attention to the great importance of the new (in this century) class of older middle-aged adults. He says that our present conceptions and social structures assume that early adulthood (that is, up to age forty or forty-five) is the crucial period of life, as it was in previous times when only a small proportion of the population lived on to their fifties and sixties. As a result, *many* people in late middle adulthood lack a clear self-concept and sense of meaning and purpose in life. Levinson offers a valuable application of phase theory in calling for societal measures to give older middle-aged adults greater self-respect and integrate them better into mainstream culture.

In conclusion, then, there are important and often widespread changes which take place during adulthood, and accordingly it is appropriate to attempt to develop accurate accounts of adult phases. Further, even existing phase theories, though flawed, are worthy of attention since they offer some insights, especially into what *might* happen in adulthood as distinct from what inevitably will happen. However, it is crucial that phase accounts be *strictly qualified* so they don't go beyond the facts and mislead us, whether about our own future or about the future of others. Also, it is essential that we look not only for changes but also for elements which remain largely unchanged throughout life. These can have just as much significance as changes. The almost exclusive preoccupation with change in research into adult life has had unfortunate consequences for both theory and practice. In Chapter 8 we will look at some of the many ways in which value preoccupations and personality traits tend to stay the same during the adult years.

CHAPTER 7

Stages of Adult Development: Improvement with Age?

We have seen that Levinson, Sheehy, and Erikson, while outlining psychosocial "seasons" and "passages" in adulthood, also assume that on the whole there is improvement with age. That is, they present a stage theory as well as a phase theory. Other writers, whom I will call stage theorists, are even more explicit in maintaining that there is average *improvement* with age. In this chapter, we will look at the nature, problems, and potential usefulness of stage theories, concentrating especially on the work of Lawrence Kohlberg and (to a lesser extent) James Fowler.[1]

1. Some of the material in this chapter is taken, with permission and modification, from my paper "Is There Really Development? An Alternative Interpretation," *The Journal of Moral Education* **18**, 3 (October 1989), pp. 174-85.

The Claim That Higher (and Older) Is Better

Lawrence Kohlberg, building on the work of Piaget, has proposed six stages of moral development as follows:

Stage 1 – Punishment and Obedience Orientation
Stage 2 – Individual Instrumental Purpose and Exchange
Stage 3 – Mutual Interpersonal Expectations, Relationships, and Conformity
Stage 4 – Social System and Conscience Maintenance
Stage 5 – Prior Rights and Social Contract or Utility
Stage 6 – Universal Ethical Principles[2]

Kohlberg's theory, based on extensive empirical studies, is that all people pass sequentially through these stages. While few (if any) attain Stage 6 and only a small minority reach a full Stage 5, insofar as people develop morally they do so through these stages and in this order. And of those who reach a particular stage, few if any regress.

Although Kohlberg's theory is about stages rather than ages, he does establish "age norms," especially in childhood and adolescence, but also to a degree in adulthood. For example, he says that the pre-conventional level of morality (Stages 1 and 2) "is usually occupied by children aged four to ten";[3] and that virtually no one attains substantial Stage 5 usage (the first post-conventional stage) by the end of high school. Stage 5, he says, insofar as it occurs at all, "is an adulthood stage"; until their late twenties people simply have not had life experience of the

2. L. Kohlberg, *The Philosophy of Moral Development* (San Francisco: Harper and Row, 1981), pp. 409-412.
3. *Ibid.*, p. 16.

kind required to reach Stage 5: "experiences of adult responsibility are conditions involved in the movement to principled moral thought."[4] In a book on moral development which was assessed favorably by Kohlberg, further age trends are provided as follows:

Ages 13 – 14	Stage 2/3 is predominant, with Stages 1/2 and 2 falling off rapidly and Stage 3 emerging.
Ages 16 – 18	Stage 3 is predominant, with Stages 1/2 and 2 continuing to fall off, Stage 2/3 falling off rapidly and Stage 3/4 emerging strongly.[5]

Of course, these are simply trends, and some individuals may remain at Stage 1 or 2 all their lives. However, it is clear that the Kohlberg school sees a correlation between age and stage, especially at the younger age levels.

James Fowler also assumes a link between age and what he calls "stages of faith." Faith, for Fowler, "is not always religious in its content or context."[6] Rather, it is "a person's or a group's way of moving into the force field of life. It is our way of finding coherence and giving meaning to the multiple forces and relations that make up our lives" (p. 4). "Faith is an orientation of the total person, giving purpose and goal to one's hopes and strivings, thoughts and actions" (p. 14). "Faith . . . grasps the ultimate conditions of our existence, unifying them into a comprehensive image in light of which we shape our responses and initiatives, our action" (p. 25). On

4. L. Kohlberg, *The Psychology of Moral Development* (San Francisco: Harper and Row, 1984), pp. 451-59.
5. J. Reimer, D. Paolitto, and R. Hersh, *Promoting Moral Growth: From Piaget to Kohlberg,* 2nd ed. (London: Longman, 1983), p. 100.
6. J. Fowler, *Stages of Faith: The Psychology of Human Development and the Quest for Meaning* (San Francisco: Harper and Row, 1981), p. 4.

Fowler's account, then, faith is a general outlook and response to life, including a meaning and value system. Among other things, it incorporates the stages of moral development outlined by Kohlberg. Fowler speaks of "the correlations we find between Piaget's and Kohlberg's stages . . . (and) the forms of knowing and valuing that make up a faith stage" (p. 99). And he endorses Kohlberg's claim that "more developed structural stages of knowing are, in important ways, more comprehensive and adequate than the less developed ones" (p. 101). While maintaining that Kohlberg's concerns are too narrowly cognitive (pp. 101-105), Fowler nevertheless includes Kohlberg's moral stages without alteration in his formulation of faith stages (pp. 244-45).

According to Fowler, our "faith" (in his sense) typically becomes more adequate as we grow older. He identifies six stages of faith and attaches age periods to most of them: Stage 1: Intuitive-Projective Faith (Early Childhood); Stage 2: Mythic-Literal Faith (School Years); Stage 3: Synthetic-Conventional Faith (Adolescence); Stage 4: Individuative-Reflective Faith (Young Adulthood); Stage 5: Conjunctive Faith (Mid-Life and Beyond); Stage 6: Universalizing Faith (p. 113). While Fowler does not give a specific age period for Stage 6, his sequential theory requires that it come after Stage 5 and hence in the later years of life. He describes it as "mature faith in relation to which we have sought for developmentally related prior or preparatory stages" (p. 199). Stage 6 is the "normative endpoint, the culminating image of mature faith" (p. 199).

Fowler says there is not a complete correspondence between age and stage. The age periods given are those which are "optimal" for the emergence of the corresponding stages: one may not in fact attain the stage at the age in question. He states, for example, that "ordinarily . . . Synthetic-Conventional faith does not take (full) form during adolescence"; rather, this is "the culminating form of faith for the first era of the life cycle" (p. 112). However, despite slippage of this kind, a strong *average* correlation between age and stage remains. This is guaranteed by the fact that while faith stage attainment may occur later than the "optimal" age, it can't occur earlier in any satisfactory form. Just as serious problems are created "when the anachronism of a lagging faith stage fails to keep pace with psychosocial growth," so too there will be "crippled psychosocial functioning" in those cases where "precocious faith development outstrips or gets ahead of psychosocial growth" (p. 114).

Both Kohlberg and Fowler attempt to deal explicitly with the issue of higher (and hence older) as better. Kohlberg says, for example: "From a moral point of view, the moral worth of all people is ultimately the same; it is equal . . . . The claim that Stage 6 is a more moral way of thinking is not an assignment of higher moral worth to the Stage 6 individual."[7] And Fowler says: "Faith stages . . . are not to be understood as an achievement scale by which to evaluate the worth of persons" (p. 114). These remarks parallel Erikson's statement, noted in the previous chapter, that writers who see his stages in terms of progressively higher levels of achievement have misunderstood his theory. However, in the case of all three theorists, such disclaimers don't fit with the general drift of their writings. The higher stages and the ways of life associated with them are presented in such laudatory terms that we must assume a claim that they are better. Further, they are associated with outstanding figures — Gandhi, Martin Luther King, Mother Teresa, for example — whose lives are generally taken to be exemplary. People perhaps should not be *blamed* for failing to attain the higher stages; and people of lower moral,

7. In "Stages of Moral Development as a Basis for Moral Education," in *Moral Education: Interdisciplinary Approaches*, eds. C. Beck, B. Crittenden, and E. Sullivan (Toronto: University of Toronto Press, 1971), p. 54.

psychosocial, or faith stages should be treated with respect and decency as human beings: their "moral worth" should not be called into question. But the whole thrust of the respective theories is that the higher levels are more "inclusive," "mature," and "adequate," and that the people who have attained them are superior morally, psychosocially, and so forth. Fowler states that the stages do not present "educational or therapeutic goals toward which to hurry people" (p. 114). However, this is not because these goals are not higher but rather because (on Fowler's view) they can't be reached at an earlier age, and attempts to foster them prematurely will do more harm than good.

In closing this section we should note that there is perhaps some disparity between Kohlberg's and Fowler's views on the relation between age and stage. Fowler's position is somewhat eclectic, drawing heavily on both Kohlberg and Erikson without making clear how the differences between the two are to be resolved. As we have seen, Erikson postulates definite age periods during which, all being well, the successive stages of development occur; whereas Kohlberg allows for considerable variability by age, especially in adulthood. Fowler appears to move back and forth between a Kohlbergian and an Eriksonian approach to this question. Nevertheless, one may safely say that the general thrust of their views is similar, and that for Fowler and Kohlberg alike there is average improvement in morality with age.

An Alternative View: Change Rather Than Improvement

In this section, I wish to argue that Kohlberg and Fowler (along with Erikson, Levinson, Sheehy, and others) are mistaken in seeing a correlation between age and level of human functioning. Such a position reflects the "age-ist" and "progress" biases and ideologies of our culture. I would advocate instead a strict "phase" theory, according to which the various passages of life (insofar as they exist at all) involve change rather than improvement.

It is worth noting that there have been respected traditions of thought which have seen a typical *decline* in attitudes and values with age, at least from early childhood to early adulthood. Within Christianity, for example, there are New Testament statements about the exemplary outlooks of children. Jean-Jacques Rousseau in *Emile* appears to see the child as born good and being steadily corrupted by society, unless given a very unusual upbringing. And from the progressive education tradition we have this statement by John Dewey:

> The child is born with a natural desire to give out, to do, to serve. When this tendency is not used, when conditions are such that other motives are substituted, the accumulation of an influence working against the social spirit is much larger than we have any idea of . . . .
>
> But lack of cultivation of the social spirit is not all. Positively individualistic motives and standards are inculcated.[8]

While it is useful, however, in our progress-oriented age to reflect on these alternative views, it is just as inappropriate to romanticize childhood and youth as to denigrate it. A simplistic (though favorable) conception of children, adolescents, and young adults can ultimately have negative consequences. If adults decide (as they so often do) that childlike sympathy and youthful idealism, though admirable in a way, are not fit for the "real world" and don't provide a solid basis for a "mature"

8. J. Dewey, *Moral Principles in Education* (Carbondale, Illinois: Arcturus Paperback, Southern Illinois University Press, 1975), pp. 22-23.

way of life, they may come to regard younger people as naive, immature, and psychosocially inadequate.

The view I wish to advocate is that younger people (and here I include young adults) are neither more nor less competent morally and psychosocially than older people. Changes in value outlooks with age of the kind documented by developmentalists are to be seen not as improvements but rather as adaptations to changing life circumstances.

The life situation of people in modern Western society alters to some extent with age, requiring corresponding value shifts. This is especially marked in the transition from early childhood to early adulthood, as people move from extreme dependence to a significant degree of independence; from sexual deprivation to relative sexual freedom; from being under the authority of adults to being comparatively free and perhaps in authority over one's own children; from moving in a restricted circle to having a wide circle of friends and acquaintances; from being "care-free" to having many responsibilities. But there are similarly changes from early to late adulthood, also calling for a somewhat different — but not therefore better — value system and approach to life.

Children are often criticized for placing undue emphasis on obedience, reward, and punishment in moral matters; and for tending to ignore adult moral rules when they feel they can get away with it. However, given their heavy dependence on adults and the manner in which moral rules are imposed on them largely without consultation or explanation, such an approach to *adult* morality seems quite appropriate. Children sense that this morality is biased somewhat toward adult needs and reference groups, and so view it with distrust. They must take adult definitions of "right" and "wrong" very seriously along with associated rewards and punishments: "wrong" in this sense largely means "that which is punished." However, having placed children in this position, it is perverse then to accuse them of having a distorted view of morality and, furthermore, of being incapable of anything better. In fact, children as "moral philosophers" (to use Kohlberg's description of them) do have a moral system of their own parallel to that of adults: they have ideas about what constitutes fairness, kindness, honesty, and decency, although they may not use these terms. However, the nature and expression of their morality is adapted to their distinctive socio-political reality. Further, the complexity and ingenuity of their value system must be equal to that of adults in order to solve their special problems.

Adolescents for their part are frequently accused of risk-taking, excessive experimentation, and what adults refer to as "carelessness." This set of characteristics perhaps gives rise to more anxiety and aggravation with respect to adolescents than any other. Expressions of it sometimes include drug and alcohol use, dangerous driving, relatively indiscriminate and "careless" sexual behavior, neglect of schooling, and petty criminal behavior. However, the reasons for adolescent "rebellion" and experimentation are many, and are very often valid, given the life situation of adolescents. In the first place, there is the need, frequently noted by psychologists, to create a distinctive identity and way of life through unusual and extreme forms of behavior. Second, there is an understandable curiosity to find out as much as possible about oneself and the world. Third, while adults are concerned to protect the "investment" (in the best sense of the word) they have made in raising their children, young people do not have a comparable interest and so are more prepared to take risks with their life and faculties. Fourth, young people have a sense, based partly in reality, that if they make mistakes they have the time, energy, and resources to rectify or compensate for them later in life. Fifth, the "carelessness" of young people is partly due to the fact that they don't have a major position of responsibility in society — they are dependent and have no dependents — and so they often don't have sufficiently strong reasons to be careful. Certainly they are not rewarded for being "responsible" to the degree that adults are. And finally, risk-taking behavior may arise out of a desire to avoid boredom and bring some excitement and at least fleeting meaning to a way of life that sometimes seems to have insufficient purpose in the scheme of things. For all these reasons, then, much of the behavior of adolescents which invites the charge (from adults) of immorality or amorality is based solidly on a rationale that is inherent in their life circumstances.

Young adults, too, as we saw in Chapter 6, have been described as relatively lacking in various qualities; notably, balance, self-sufficiency, wholeness, integrity, and authenticity. Only in late adulthood, according to Erikson, can we enter into "the ego's accrued assurance of its proclivity for order and meaning" and attain "post-narcissistic love" and a "spiritual sense."[9] In Levinson's view, "it is not possible to form an ideally satisfactory life structure the first time around": in early adulthood, "we are too young, inexperienced and torn . . . to resolve the contradictions."[10] Citing Jung, Levinson claims that "until the late thirties . . . a man's life is of necessity rather one-sided"; only in middle adulthood is it possible "to strengthen the formerly weaker functions and lead a more balanced life."[11]

On the one hand, however, such an analysis of younger adults is misleading in that it is unduly optimistic about what is possible in middle and late adulthood. Is there *any* age at which people typically "form an

9. E. Erikson, *Childhood and Society*, 2nd ed. (New York: Norton, 1963), p. 268.
10. D. Levinson, *The Seasons of a Man's Life* (New York: Ballantine Books, 1978), p. 82.
11. *Ibid.*, p. 33.

ideally satisfactory life structure" and "resolve the contradictions" of life? Middle adulthood, as many writers have observed, is often a period not of balance but of turmoil, indecision, and despair. And in late adulthood there are further problems with which one must struggle and new elements which one must incorporate in order to achieve balance. It would seem that, typically, *every* age's life structure is just moderately satisfactory for the life phase one is in: we shouldn't single out early adulthood for unfavorable comment in this respect. We might recall here that most of Levinson's subjects were aged between thirty-five and forty-seven when the main interviewing took place and accordingly had only limited information to offer about the middle adulthood period (age 40–60). There is a tendency when examining a particular age-group to exaggerate its problems by contrast with those of other age-groups which one hasn't in fact studied. This phenomenon is seen, for example, in the case of child psychologists who document assiduously the blind spots and irrationalities of children without sufficiently acknowledging that similar shortcomings could, with adequate study, be found in adults.

On the other hand, those who criticize young adults often fail to recognize sufficiently the *reasons* that lie behind the early adulthood mode of life. A relatively fragmented way of life is *appropriate* for younger adults, both because they can afford to take more risks and have more loose ends at this early stage, and because they are still adding elements to their life, trying to make it as full and rich as they can before a reduction in energy and time forces them to cut back. A degree of integration is necessary in every life phase if one is to achieve anything at all; but integration is not an absolute value: one cannot argue that the more integrated one's life is the better. At times there should be a greater emphasis on extension and at other times on integration. And similar points could be made about autonomy and self-sufficiency, the qualities emphasized especially by Sheehy. As Carol Gilligan and other feminist writers have commented, excessive autonomy can militate against relationships, which for most people (and, Erikson would say, especially young adults) are crucial to the good life. A degree of self-sufficiency is obviously important, but how much emphasis it should receive depends on one's needs and circumstances in a given life phase.

We see, then, that while in modern Western society values tend to *change* in certain respects with age, there is not overall *improvement*. In some ways younger people are more selfish than older people, but in other ways less so. In some ways young people have a more parochial outlook than other people, but in other ways less so. Some of the behavior of younger people is very inconvenient for older people, but the converse is also true; and in each case there are usually sincerely held and at least partly valid reasons for the behavior.

The notion that older people are superior to younger people in their value outlooks and behavior is usually based on the assumption that later stage people incorporate the strengths of earlier stages while sloughing off the weaknesses. On this view, development is cumulative, and *later* stages clearly must be *better*. We saw in Chapter 6 that this is Erikson's view; and equally it is Kohlberg's position. However, while this may happen with some individuals, many people at later stages go to an unfortunate extreme with their new emphases, and neglect important earlier values. Some of Gilligan's work, for example, would suggest that the more universalistic "justice" orientation of Kohlberg's "higher" stages can lead one to underemphasize the importance of the small-scale "networking" and "caring" characteristic of Stage

3.[12] And David Gauthier has proposed that Kohlberg's conventional stages (3 and 4) are a kind of cul-de-sac of extreme conformism one unfortunately gets into (presumably through overly heavy socialization) and one must return in part to the more sensible instrumental position of Stage 2 and build a sophisticated moral outlook on that foundation.[13]

While I would not deny that older people in fact retain to a degree the insights of earlier phases, equally I believe that younger people already have in some form the insights of later phases. As a result, there are a wide range of talents at each level. Young people (including young adults) who appear as Stage 1, 2, or 3 on Kohlberg's scale, for example, recognize in certain ways the importance of rules, law and order, social contracts, human rights, fundamental principles, and respect for persons — the so-called "distinctive insights" of later stages. If they did not, their moral competence might indeed be less than that of people who test at Stage 4, 5, or 6. However, they entertain and apply these insights in a form adapted to their socio-political situation — in such a form, by the way, that the insights may not be detected by an interviewer using later adult categories. The view I am advocating is *somewhat* like the one presented by Erikson, noted in Chapter 6. He remarks that "each critical item of psychosocial strength discussed here is systematically related to all others . . . and . . . each item exists in some form before its critical time normally arrives." He says further that "they all must exist from the beginning in some form, for every act calls for an integration of all."[14] However, Erikson's position is that

12. C. Gilligan, *In a Different Voice* (Cambridge, MA: Harvard University Press, 1982), *passim*.
13. In C. Beck et al., *Moral Education: Interdisciplinary Approaches*, p. 365.
14. *Childhood and Society*, p. 271.

after the "critical time" arrives each "new" virtue is attained in a much *fuller* form than before, so that in a well-functioning human being there is steady improvement with age in overall psychosocial capacity. This is clearly contrary to the position for which I have argued.

It may be possible, then, to save Kohlberg's (and Fowler's) Stages 1 to 4 by seeing them as *descriptive* of shifting *emphases* within a *common* set of values as children, adolescents, and adults experience (or choose) changing life circumstances which require a somewhat modified value system. Such an understanding of Kohlberg's theory would enable us to retain many of its descriptive insights while rejecting its progress and age-ist assumptions. However, it would involve a major reinterpretation of the theory.

An even more radical reinterpretation of Kohlberg's (and Fowler's) moral development theory would be needed to save Stages 5 and 6, his "post-conventional" level. These cannot be seen as descriptive, in my view, because they do not involve mere adaptation to changing circumstances but rather a more moral point of view that would be appropriate at any age and in any circumstances. On Kohlberg's view, Stage 6 incorporates the principles of universality and impartiality. Stage 5 is characterized by much greater complexity in moral thought than previous stages and a giant step in the direction of a universalistic ethic of the Stage 6 type. Now, while one may not wish to accept full universality and impartiality in Kohlberg's sense (for reasons discussed in Chapter 5 above), clearly a globally-oriented ethic of some kind is needed (again for reasons given in Chapter 5); and certainly we need a complex ethic which as far as possible takes account of all relevant considerations (for reasons presented in Chapter 2). But such an ethic — complex and globally responsible — is accessible to *all* people, young and old, including those who are descriptively at Stage 1, 2, 3, or 4 by virtue of their life circumstances. On this view, "post-conventional" morality would not be "post" in a temporal sense. Rather, it would represent a balanced, integrated, and globally-oriented perspective which, among other things, overcomes the *potential* extremes of Stages 1 to 4. Thus one could have, for example, distinctive Stage 2 emphases, appropriate to a younger child's life situation in our type of society, and yet a highly developed (for example, Stage 5) awareness of the range of considerations one must weigh in moral decision making. Whether any developmentalist of the Kohlberg or Fowler schools would be able or willing to adopt such an interpretation of the highest stages of morality is uncertain. I offer it to show that there is much that is worth salvaging in what Kohlberg and Fowler are talking about at this level, but that it must be salvaged for younger as well as older people.

What I am claiming is that there is not, on average, improvement in values with age. The qualification "on average" is, of course, very important. I don't wish to deny that *some* older people are more moral than the average younger person; all I wish to deny is that older people are in general superior to younger people in value matters.

Changes in value emphases related to changes in life situation are of course important, since if one does not achieve them one will be in serious trouble personally and will create problems for others. An adult fixated at Stage 2 is usually a sorry sight. But they are like the changes in pattern of life one must make when moving from a small rural community to a large city. There is no sense in which the latter pattern is superior to the former: it's just different. Both represent an appropriate response to one's life situation. If one tried to live in the city exactly as one had in the country, one would be in trouble.

It may seem odd that human beings don't develop better values as they grow older, since in many areas they do improve with age. For several years after reaching middle childhood, for example, people in our society are progressively able to run faster, swim further, write more quickly, read more "difficult" material, perform a wider range of mathematical calculations, and so on. However, we should note that there are other areas in which we do *not* typically improve with age: for example, in learning foreign languages, in relating to our peers, and in coping with life. It would be strange to say that adults in general "cope better" than children: adults seem to have at least as many coping problems as children. Whether or not there is average improvement with age, then, depends very much on the nature of the capacity in question. Value capacity, it seems to me, is more like coping ability than it is like mathematical ability. Mathematical ability has to do with a very narrow band of skills involved in the manipulation of numbers, which can be and typically are taught in a specialized and intensive manner. Values, by contrast, have to do with large segments of one's general approach to life. People on average (in Western society) get more and more on top of doing mathematical calculations, at least until their early teens; but they don't on average get more and more on top of life as they grow older.

At some time in the future it may be established that one age group is marginally superior to other age groups in its value orientation. (Just as it may be established that one sex or one race has marginally better values than another.) However, at present no such finding is in; and the consequences of assuming such superiority (as with gender and race) are so glaringly unfortunate that we must avoid such assumptions. The harmful effects in terms of bad inter-age relations and poor educational practice are perhaps the most obvious. But we should also note that such a theory sets us off on a wild goose chase in our inquiry into values in adulthood, leading us to assume differences that don't exist and neglect other phenomena which require urgent attention.

Is Improvement Possible?

If people don't on average improve in value matters as they grow older, what is the point of teaching or learning values in adulthood? And what hope is there for people who have confusions and difficulties in the value area and would like to overcome them?

These questions, though natural enough, show a misunderstanding of the implications of the foregoing discussion. The point is not that value improvement is impossible, but rather that it doesn't take place differentially along age lines. Also, while older people are not on average superior to younger people (or vice versa), a *particular* older (or younger) adult can progress in value matters and rise above the average. Again, a *particular* society or community can move to a higher level of value functioning, even though within that society or community there will not be an average superiority of one age-group over another.

The reason that adequacy of values does not correlate with age is twofold: (a) value solutions are largely arrived at by communal experimentation, so that all the people involved in achieving a solution — young and old alike — have knowledge of it and participate in applying it; and (b) insofar as effective new techniques of values learning and teaching are found, they can be (and typically are) applied as much to younger people as to older people.

A community of older adults, living in isolation (for example, a colony of Buddhist monks), could conceivably achieve an unusually high level of value functioning and an unusually good way of life. (A group of young adults or children might do the same, given the opportunity.) However, insofar as older people live in community with younger people, they have shared value problems with those younger people and shared successes in resolving them which are (and must be) disseminated throughout the community. The solutions, by their very nature, cannot be discovered separately by the older members of the community and subsequently taught (or not taught) to the younger members. The solutions either permeate the community or are not achieved at all.

While the communal nature of values learning restricts the extent to which individuals and sub-groups can move ahead of their culture and society, there is *some* room for individual differences. Some people will grasp better and implement more fully the solutions arrived at, and also invent some of their own. However, once again, there will be as many younger people as older people among those who move ahead in this way: there is no reason why older people should in general have greater competence or willingness in this regard.

Particularly wise and talented teachers of values, too, may emerge and be appreciated by the society as a whole. But they may be older or younger members of the society. At present it is unusual for people in early adulthood to be recognized as great social and moral teachers. However, in my view this is largely due to the current value prejudice against adolescents and younger adults and the lack of opportunity given them to become established as leaders and teachers. Also, younger people, being in certain respects an "oppressed" group, tend to internalize the opinions of them held by their elders and, as a result, lack the confidence to become teachers of values.[15]

15. The position I am arguing against here is that older adults are superior to younger adults, since that is the point of view taken by the theorists we are considering. We should not forget, however, that people in late adulthood, too, are sometimes ignored as teachers of values because they are thought to be *too* old. This, equally, is a mistake.

But while improvement in values *is* possible (for young and old alike), this doesn't mean that it is easy, or that it is the only task with which we should be concerned as we grow older. It is quite an achievement simply to sustain a steady level of sound values and well-being. Even *at* a particular age, new problems keep emerging which require new insights or new applications of old insights. And as we go on to new phases of adult life with their new challenges, once again we have to work hard to maintain our present level of value adequacy. In many ways we have been *too* improvement-oriented in the field of values, due to a combination of a progress notion of adult development and a perfectionist view of humanity. Certainly we should strive for improvement. But if we are too preoccupied with it, we may not sufficiently appreciate and enjoy our lives as they currently are; and we may seriously neglect the maintenance of a good way of life in the fanatical (and vain) pursuit of a perfect life.

The Problems and Potential Usefulness of Stage Theories

Some of the problems of stage theories have already been mentioned. Perhaps the most obvious is that younger people are discriminated against on the ground that they have inferior values. They are treated with less respect, their judgments are not taken seriously in arriving at decisions (if indeed they are consulted at all), and they are often automatically excluded from certain roles and positions.

A closely related problem is that relationships between younger and older people are typically undermined by the latter's sense of superiority. We are all familiar with cases where parent–child relationships are spoiled by parents' constant attempts to impose their values (which they assume to be superior) on their children, a phenomenon which often continues until the "children" are well into middle age. Similar difficulties arise between teachers and students, bosses and junior employees, senior and junior colleagues. Enormous potential for warm, productive relationships is lost simply because it is assumed that the values of younger people are inferior.

Another problem is that stage theories, like phase theories, often lead to stereotyping. It is easy to assume that everyone who is at Stage 2, for example, has the same value outlook, whereas in fact there may be considerable variation. As we will discuss at greater length in Chapter 8, certain traits — relative selfishness, generosity, possessiveness, reliability, and so on — tend to persist in particular people throughout life, regardless of their general test results on a morality or "faith" inventory. Such individual differences, while acknowledged to some extent, are usually not highlighted in stage theories.

A further problem with stage theories is that they limit our expectations of people at particular stages and ages. This has been widely touted as an advantage of stage theories. Piaget, for example, is seen as coming to the rescue of cognitively immature children who have been unduly "pressured" by the school system; and Kohlberg's ideas are thought to make us more tolerant of the moral foibles of children and teenagers. But if in fact young people *are* as capable of having sound values as older people, as I have argued, it does them a disservice to refrain from challenging them to confront fundamental value issues. A parallel might be drawn here with assuming that females are genetically less capable of scientific and mathematical thought than males and so "protecting" them from demanding studies or jobs in these areas.

So far I have focussed especially on the difficulties created by seeing younger people as less competent in value matters than older people. However, another set of problems has to do with viewing certain categories of people as less "mature" than others, regardless of age.

Carol Gilligan has discussed the tendency to see females as less morally competent than males because of a presumed difference in their emphasis on principles and, in particular, the value of justice.[16] Other invidious comparisons, unrelated to age, are also made. For example, adults of lower socio-economic status, lower educational level, and less "liberal" religious affiliation are often judged to be at a lower stage of moral judgment.[17] As with age prejudice, bias along gender, class, educational, and religious lines is both mistaken and inimical to good relations and productive co-operation among people of different categories in a society and globally. Of course, it is not essential that stage theories should discriminate against whole categories of people in this way, but experience to date shows that the danger is very real.

Becoming more positive, we should look also at the potential usefulness of stage theories when their stage-improvement assumptions are taken away. To begin with, such theories can, as we noted earlier, be viewed as *descriptive* accounts of distinctive emphases in values at different age levels in childhood, adolescence, and early adulthood. In this respect, they are like phase theories, describing "passages" that young people go through, without assuming that change of emphasis means improvement. The huge volume of empirical data gathered by developmentalists can be sifted and used with a different interpretation to inform us about the moral and faith life of children, youth, and young adults. Of course, on the account I have given, there are many other insights that young people have which developmentalists have

16. C. Gilligan, *In a Different Voice, passim.*
17. J. Rest, *Development in Judging Moral Issues* (Minneapolis: University of Minnesota Press, 1979), pp. 111-16.

overlooked and which must be incorporated into the total picture.[18]

Again, the research of developmentalists has revealed not only phases young people *do* go through, but also phases they *must* go through in order to adapt well to their constantly changing socio-political circumstances in modern Western society. Stage theorists are mistaken in saying that one normally must move up stages in order to improve one's morality; but it is nevertheless true that one must move through the stages (to Stage 3 or 4, at any rate) in order to *continue* to function well as one grows older and is assigned different responsibilities and permitted different types of relationships.

Further, stage theory has served to identify different *types* of value system, which may occur at various ages. Although, in my view, it is a mistake to see Stage 4 as superior to Stage 3, the detailed description of these value outlooks offered by Kohlberg and others provides fascinating material for study. How much overlap is there between these orientations; what circumstances and needs would lead a person to adopt one emphasis rather than another as a permanent approach to life in adulthood; what are the respective strengths and potential weaknesses of the two outlooks? These and other questions can be pursued with the benefit of the extensive empirical material that has been gathered.

A further contribution of stage theory has been to help uncover not only different types of value system but also different components *within* a person's value system. As indicated, I believe that all the value elements highlighted by the successive stages in Kohlberg's and Fowler's

18. Readers are referred here to two important works which have studied childhood from a non-adult-supremacist perspective in the fields of morality and religion respectively: R. Coles, *The Moral Life of Children* (Boston: Atlantic Monthly Press, 1986), and E. Robinson, *The Original Vision* (New York: Seabury Press, 1983).

accounts are present from childhood onward: they simply take on different forms and are given different emphases with movement through the stages. However, identification of the components is useful. Even if one rejects the stage-improvement assumption, then, the detailed empirical description of these components can be utilized in arriving at a deeper understanding of people's value structures.

Finally, stage theories are of value in that they remind us of the possibility of improvement in values. While improvement may not be age-linked, as stage theorists have claimed, an individual at a given age can achieve a more adequate value system; and a whole community, including all age groups, can improve their values. Again, while developmentalists have exaggerated the extent to which value improvement in one area is related to improvement in other areas, certainly improvement in particular areas — for example, religious tolerance, treatment of children, environmental ethics, and so on — is possible, and there is indeed *some* connection between different value areas. Thus, despite the errors to date in the way in which value development has been characterized, the basic project of determining how value improvement takes place and how it can be accelerated is worth supporting, provided improvement is not seen as related to age.

CHAPTER 8

Change and Continuity in Adult Life

In Chapters 6 and 7, criticisms were presented of theories which exaggerate change in adulthood. However, some change does indeed take place during the adult years. The time has come to outline more systematically ways in which adults change and remain the same, focussing especially on values.

The purpose of studying patterns of change and continuity was noted in the previous chapters. It helps us see which changes we can expect or can assist to happen, and which ones are so unlikely that to expect them or attempt to bring them about is normally a mistake.

A key to success in adult living is to "go with the flow" in the Taoist sense: to strike a direction amid the currents of life which recognizes natural forces and impediments.[1] Some struggle is of course necessary, but

1. H. Smith, *The Religions of Man* (New York: Harper and Row, Perennial Library, 1965), pp. 204-207.

as Hans Selye has said, we should avoid fights we cannot win.[2] This requires constant inquiry into the possibilities and impossibilities of adult change. The present chapter is an introduction to this inquiry.

Change in Values

Phase theorists have concentrated on adult changes which (in their view) are universal or almost so. In this section I will begin by looking at changes of that kind, but go on to note changes of a type largely neglected by theorists: ones which are typical only of certain sub-groups or which happen only to some individuals.

(a) *Universal (and almost Universal) Changes*

There are some changes in values and related matters which occur to all or virtually all human beings around the globe as they pass from early to late adulthood. The following are some highlights. It should be noted that these changes usually take place gradually, over a long period of time, and are shifts of degree and emphasis rather than abrupt changes.

1. Almost universally, in adolescence and early adulthood there is a gradual change from heavy dependence on and closeness to our original family to the establishing of our own intimate circle (which may still include our parents but in a different configuration). Then, later in life, our parents grow older, perhaps become dependent on us in certain ways, and eventually die. These changes in family relationships modify our values, responsibilities, and self-image. Some of these changes are captured by the phase theorists' concept of "increasing autonomy."[3] However, some writers (for example, Carol Gilligan) are

2. H. Selye, *Stress Without Distress* (New York: Signet, New American Library, 1974), pp. 37-41.
3. G. Sheehy, *Passages* (New York: Bantam, 1976), pp. 36, 48-49.

concerned about the separation implied by the term autonomy, and prefer to speak of a transition from dependence to interdependence: relationships change but do not necessarily diminish in closeness or importance.[4]

2. During adulthood, we gradually shift from an expansive, risk-taking phase to an integrative, meaning-making phase. In later adulthood, much of our attention is given to reorganizing, reinterpreting, or making the most of the components in our lives rather than adding new ones (although that obviously continues). We are still learning many new things, but increasingly within an established framework. This emphasis on integration is alluded to in phase theorists' work — notably Erikson's — by reference to the synthesis and "integrity" achieved in late adulthood.[5]

3. Outside the family, as well as within it, we change from having older people "above" us to having younger people "below" us, not only chronologically but in community, workplace, and other roles. We have to adjust to thinking of ourselves as an older person instead of a younger person, and accept the changing images and functions this implies in our culture. Erikson speaks of our responsibility for "generativity" in middle age, for contributing to society and establishing a legacy.[6] Levinson discusses the complex transition from having mentors to serving as a mentor to others.[7]

4. We move from having most of our life before us to having most of it behind us. This requires a significant

4. C. Gilligan, *In a Different Voice* (Cambridge, Mass.: Harvard University Press, 1982), pp. 73-75.
5. See E. Erikson, *Childhood and Society*, 2nd ed. (New York: Norton, 1963), pp. 268-69; and E. Erikson et al., *Vital Involvement in Old Age* (New York: Norton, 1986), pp. 70-71.
6. *Childhood and Society*, pp. 266-68.
7. D. Levinson, *The Seasons of Man's Life* (New York: Ballantine Books, 1978), pp. 251-54.

adjustment in perspective. It can result in panic, a sense of "running out of time" as documented by Levinson (pp. 139, 192), or simply a determination to be more selective about what we do, taking advantage of the fact that we now have a better idea of what fits, what we are capable of and enjoy, what fulfils our goals and gives meaning to our life.

5. We become increasingly aware of limits to what we can achieve in life, of what form our life has taken and must take as distinct from what it might take. This can lead, in Levinson's terms, to "loss of our dream," to "de-illusionment" (or disillusionment) (pp. 192-93). Even if we fulfil our dreams in some sense, we may find the experience disappointing and rather different from what we had expected. New values and rationalizations must be developed in order to sustain a sense of purpose and meaning.

6. With increasing age, there is typically a growing incidence of health problems, and physical decline and limitation become more apparent. The impact of this on our way of life has been exaggerated, but is nevertheless significant. Certain activities must be curtailed and there is likely to be a greater preoccupation with health and fitness. This need not reduce the quality of our lives, but some adjustments in our values and pursuits must be made.

7. We tend to attach greater value to security as we grow older. This is partly because, as noted earlier, we are trying to protect and elaborate a good way of life we have established rather than create something new. It is also due to the possibility that sickness and/or unemployment due to age may reduce our capacity to fend for ourselves. Also, if things go wrong we have less time to repair them.

8. In later adulthood, death comes to more of our "significant others," and our own *certain* ultimate death (as distinct from possible early or "untimely" death) becomes a more relevant consideration. Once again, while this need not reduce our enjoyment of and zest for life, it

inevitably affects our outlook and values in certain ways. We think more often of the need to "set things in order" and what we wish to achieve before we die.

(b) *Changes Characteristic of a Sub-Group*
Value changes which are not universal but are common within a sub-group are sometimes found. Most of these changes are "characteristic" or "typical" rather than invariant within the group. Here are some examples:

Socio-economic class. The value challenges and changes of people at a particular age often vary according to their social class.[8] For example, in the lower working class in modern Western societies the likelihood of having to live with chronic unemployment as a young adult and develop values necessary for that state is far greater than in the middle and upper classes. And in middle adulthood, a major life task of a lower-class person who has a steady job may be to cope with boredom at work, while a middle-class person may be struggling rather with an excess of work and the problems of "workaholism." Phase theorists have tended to focus on the lives of middle-class and (to a lesser degree) upper working-class people and to neglect the complexities of the situation of "underclass" people. Of course, even within a given class there is considerable variation in the age at which changes occur; but class-specific phase accounts can give a better sense of the direction our lives may take, depending on our class.[9]

8. See C. Kasworm, "Facilitating Ethical Development: A Paradox," in *Ethical Issues in Adult Education*, ed. R. Brockett (New York: Teachers College Press, 1988), p. 24.
9. See R. Coles, *The Moral Life of Children* (Boston: Atlantic Monthly Press, 1986), for a study of the extent to which underclass children in many countries and sub-communities must from an early age take on responsibilities and accompanying values which, in other classes, are more typical of adults.

Gender. Women's circumstances and values in modern industrialized society tend to differ in many ways from those of men, and this is reflected in the type of value shifts which take place and the age at which they occur. For example, when many men are preoccupied with making a success of their first major paying job, many women are absorbed in bearing and raising children (as well as, in many cases, coping with a job outside the home); and when some men decide to become more involved in family life (perhaps in their late thirties or early forties), many women are ready to place greater emphasis than before on occupational and other activities outside the home.[10]

Historical era. The type of changes and the age at which they occur also varies with the historical period. Already some of the age trends identified by Levinson and Sheehy in the early 1970s have become dated. As young people become more informed about adult problems, they confront them earlier and with less of a sense of shock; as youth unemployment increases, patterns of "pulling up roots" and "breaking away" from the family change; as more women take up permanent careers outside the home, receiving wages on which the family is heavily dependent, there are shifts in the type and timing of (typical) adulthood phases. And if we look at earlier decades and centuries it is even clearer how historically relative adult change can be. For example, there have been eras when "old age" occurred much earlier and when "whole manhood" (or what we might call "middle age" today) also came earlier and involved a different set of goals and challenges.[11]

10. See *Passages*, pp. 169-71. See M. Fiske and D. Chiriboga, *Change and Continuity in Adult Life* (San Francisco: Jossey-Bass, 1990), p. 279.
11. See P. Ariès, *Centuries of Childhood* (New York: Vintage Books, Random House, 1962), pp. 30-31; and Levinson, *The Seasons of a Man's Life*, pp. 326-30.

Society or culture. Adult change also varies from one society or culture to another.[12] For example, some societies revere their old people, so the loss of status and influence associated with late adulthood in modern Western societies simply does not occur. Again, societies often vary in the age at which young people are recognized as adults and admitted to full participation in the community. Yet again, societies often vary in the extent to which women participate in public life and hence experience life phases similar to those of men (for example, the traditional "student," "householder," and "retirement" phases of Indian society).

(c) *Individual Changes*

It is important to recognize the extent to which change may be an individual matter, reflecting individual differences in needs, personality, and circumstances which have nothing to do with universal or sub-group patterns. Certain changes are experienced by some people but *not at all* by others. For example, one person may maintain much the same political values throughout adult life while another may progress steadily from a conservative to a radical outlook, or vice versa. It is difficult to anticipate such idiosyncratic value change without detailed knowledge of the individual; and even then, of course, we may be surprised.

Other changes happen to virtually everyone, but the *age* at which they occur varies from person to person. We noted this in Chapter 6. For example, while all humans become concerned about their mortality, some are particularly preoccupied with it at thirty, others at fifty, and others at seventy. Again, while most people are interested in having a sexual "partner," they vary in the age at

12. See J. Hendricks and C. Hendricks, *Aging in Mass Society: Myths and Realities* (Cambridge, MA: Winthrop Publ., 1977), p. 169.

which this interest is strongest and is given particular forms of expression. A heightened "urge to merge" comes for some people at sixteen and others at thirty-six; and in some cases it leads to marriage while in others simply to a close friendship.[13] Within a particular culture age trends might be identified, but the number of exceptions even in that culture will be considerable.

The reasons for the individual differences in people's value patterns are often found in their distinctive temperaments. However, they may also be due to differences in life circumstances, or to accidents of fate. For example, people with an unhappy family life in childhood and adolescence may wish to establish their own nuclear family early as a means of escape. Again, a person who in early adulthood is faced with the death of close friends or family members will almost certainly experience at that time a special concern about values related to mortality. Yet again, people who choose to marry and have children will undergo a distinctive change in values — having to do with child rearing, schooling, nuclear family life, and so on — which other people of the same age may not experience, given their different life circumstances.

Continuity in Values

While there are changes which take place during adulthood, too often in adult psychology and education we have dwelt on change to the neglect of continuity. Increasingly today researchers and practitioners are becoming aware of ways in which adults remain the same throughout life. Patricia Cross, for example, after an extensive review of research on adult life, observes that "for most of the adult years consistency in personality is

13. Gail Sheehy outlines some of these variations in *Passages*, pp. 253-54 and 295-96.

more probable than change."[14] Hendricks and Hendricks, quoting from Neugarten, Havighurst, and Tobin, state that as people grow older "those characteristics that have been central to the personality seem to become even more clearly delineated, and those values the individual has been cherishing become even more salient."[15] Dorothy MacKeracher, in a discussion of women in late adulthood, says that successful aging occurs "when the older individual can maintain the predispositions and characteristics she developed throughout life, in spite of internal or external changes which might affect her self-identity or lifestyle."[16] And in a recent study, Kathryn Logsdail notes with respect to her late adulthood interviewees that "childhood was the primary time period discussed as the origin for value formation .... Values were perceived to have been formed from the teachings and experiences of one's childhood circumstance. They were later described as being solidified through personal reflection in dealing with new experiences ...."[17]

By way of illustrating this general point, let us look at some examples of value continuity in adult life. The particular continuities noted fall into three categories: universal, sub-group, and individual.

(a) *Universal (and almost Universal) Continuities*

I will mention two broad types of value continuity found in adulthood:

14. K. P. Cross, *Adults as Learners* (San Francisco: Jossey-Bass, 1981), p. 167.
15. *Aging in Mass Society: Myths and Realities*, p. 129.
16. D. MacKeracher, *A Study of the Experience of Aging from the Perspective of Older Women*, unpublished doctoral thesis, University of Toronto, Toronto, 1982, p. 344.
17. K. Longsdail, *The Phenomenon of Learning from Living: A Perspective on Values of Older Adults*, unpublished doctoral thesis, University of Toronto, Toronto, pp. 181-82.

Continuity in value concerns. Human beings the world over confront certain value issues continuously from early to late adulthood: How should I relate to other people? How much should I look after my own well-being and how much the well-being of others? What friendship patterns should I have? How much importance should I attach to family life? How dependent/independent should I be? How should I express/gratify my sexuality? How should I relate to people of the opposite gender and to those of the same gender? How should I relate to people of other religions, races, ethnic groups, social classes? What should I attempt to achieve in life? How should I seek to attain meaning in life? To what extent and in what ways should I concern myself with physical/ material security? To what extent and in what ways should I promote my health/fitness? What attitude should I have to physical decline as I grow older? How should I deal with the limitations of life? How should I view the fact that, sooner or later, I will die?

Different people handle these issues in different ways, and may vary somewhat in their approach to them over time. Nevertheless, the continuity of value concerns throughout life is impressive, and has been greatly underestimated by theorists who associate particular value questions almost exclusively with particular ages.

Continuity in values. As well as continuities in the value issues all human beings confront, we also find universal continuities in the actual values they have. As we saw in Chapter 2, there are certain "basic values" which are characteristic of all people from childhood to late adulthood: survival, health, happiness, friendship, helping others (to an extent), self-respect, respect from others, knowledge, freedom, fulfilment, a sense of meaning in life, and so on. Once again, while different people hold these values with somewhat different emphases, and the emphases may change to some extent over time, these values are held around the globe and continuously throughout life: they are not associated especially with particular age groups.

(b) *Continuities within a Sub-Group*

There are other continuities in values and related matters which, while going beyond the individual, are not universal. Rather, they are characteristic of many (though not all) members of a sub-group. Here are just a few examples:

Socio-economic class. People of a "lower" class in Western society must, all their lives, take steps to avoid feelings of inferiority due to their class membership. They have to be on their guard against messages in both "popular" and "high" culture which downgrade their worth. Accordingly, they value elements in society which give some recognition to their class, and activities which give them a sense of accomplishment and protect them from invidious comparisons with people of "higher" classes. These values they acquire at an early age and of necessity maintain for the rest of their lives (unless their class membership changes).

Ethnic group. Most members of a given ethnic group encounter certain typical problems, advantages, and challenges throughout life. The experience of the eight-year-old may have much in common with that of the eighty-year-old of the same ethnic membership. Accordingly, certain values tend to persist throughout life, ones which help members of the group maintain a sense of self-esteem, survive, and flourish.

Gender. From early childhood to old age, most people have a strong sense of their gender and have many of the values characteristic of their gender in their society. They confront continuing problems associated with the attitudes toward and expectations of their gender, and value those strategies, relationships, and activities which in some way alleviate these problems. For example, as we will see in Chapter 9, many of the distinctive values of women in the Western world today — for example, friendship, dialogue, caring, gentleness — are due at least in part to the need to achieve a tolerable existence for themselves in a situation of subordination and relative powerlessness.

Historical era. In particular regions of the world, various historical periods have been noted for pervasive values, such as religious prejudice, acceptance of slavery, respect for learning, prizing of military prowess, celebration of science and technology, and ecological concern. Accordingly, people who have lived in these eras (in the regions in question) have usually had these values from childhood to old age, rather than simply during a particular phase of their lives.

Society or culture. Certain values are characteristic of members of a particular society or culture. For example, a society may be distinctively traditionalist, or romantic, or materialistic, or tolerant. Insofar as individuals share the prevailing values of their society, they tend to do so from cradle to grave, since the values are inherent in the culture in which they participate.

(c) *Individual Continuities*

Despite what phase and stage theorists have said, there is remarkable continuity in moral and other value-related personality characteristics from childhood to late adulthood, differing from individual to individual. Some people are miserly all their lives, others generous or spendthrift; some are relatively caring, others often inconsiderate; some tend to be antisocial, others unable to resist socializing; some are rather selfish or "self-absorbed," others unselfish to the point of neglecting their own well-being; some are relatively insecure, others quite confident; some are cautious, others carefree or careless; some are dependent, others independent. There may be slight shifts of emphasis over time, but the continuity in a great many cases is marked.

In addition to general personality traits such as the above, there are also continuities of a more specific type, again varying from person to person. Some people care a great deal — all their lives — about the clothes they wear; others about how much money they have; others about travel; others about extending their education; others about sexual enjoyment; others about knowing what is going on in the world. Some of these values may be linked to more basic personality traits: people may value money because they are insecure, or travel because they are interested in other people. But whatever the reasons, the fact remains that idiosyncratic value continuities of this specific kind are widespread, adding to the picture of substantial continuity in values throughout adulthood.

Reasons for Continuity in Values

The tendency (noted in the preceding section) of adults to remain rather similar in many of their values throughout life requires some explanation if it is to be believed. Retention of desirable traits is understandable. But why are characteristics such as miserliness, self-absorption, and insecurity so resistant to change? And even with regard to desirable traits, why is it so difficult to become *more* generous, caring, and confident than we were earlier in life?

This topic will be dealt with at some length in later chapters, especially in Part Four. However, we might briefly note here several theories on the subject. While each theory is often presented in too strong a form, as the *sole* explanation of the phenomenon, together they provide a fairly plausible explanation of why there is so much continuity in values throughout adulthood.

To begin with, it would seem that there is a major genetic basis for personality traits. In the unending nature-versus-nurture debate, some truth undoubtedly lies with those who stress "nature" or heredity. This helps explain why children often have traits remarkably similar to those of grandparents, aunts, and uncles, and very different from those of the parents and siblings. It also, incidentally, takes some pressure off harried parents who feel personally responsible for the shortcomings of their children.

A second probable contribution to many deeply embedded personality traits is prenatal and early postnatal experience. There is increasing emphasis today on the importance of the psychological and physiological state of the mother during pregnancy, and the infant's first experiences, including those of birth itself. It seems very likely, for example, that a person's basic sense of security or insecurity, trust or mistrust is strongly influenced by experiences at this initial stage of life.

Other theorists stress the importance of early and middle childhood experience in shaping personality. In modern times, Freud has been a key exponent of the view that we are largely formed in childhood and much of the rest of our lives is necessarily a playing out of that early formation (unless a clever psychoanalyst comes to our aid). More recently, the formative nature of childhood has been emphasized by Morris Massey, who coined the phrase "What you are is where you were when"; that is, the values you have in adulthood largely reflect the characteristics of your society when you were in middle childhood (approximately age ten).[18]

Finally, according to a very different type of theory, we are resistant to change in adulthood not only because of heredity and early experiences but also because we are largely creatures of the socio-cultural *system* in which we live, and unless that changes it is extremely difficult for individuals to change. On this "systemic" view, advocated

18. M. Massey, "What You Are Is Where You Were When . . . .", a film (Chicago: Video Publishing, 1976).

notably by Emile Durkheim[19] and, recently, Michael Apple,[20] traits such as aggressiveness and a materialistic outlook are virtually forced upon us, at least to a degree, by the concepts, practices, and relationships which are taken for granted in our society. One problem with this theory is that it does not explain individual differences in values. However, it is integral to the theory that we have exaggerated the extent to which individual differences occur, and that there are in fact certain social sins (and presumably virtues) in which virtually everyone in a society shares, at least to a degree.[21]

These theories, then, help explain the phenomenon of continuity in values. However, there is also change (as we saw earlier); and much of the literature on adult development in recent times has arisen as a legitimate (though exaggerated) reaction against the notion of adulthood as *merely* a time for playing out earlier formation. We now turn to a brief consideration of how a degree of change is possible in adulthood, despite the tendency toward continuity. Once again, this issue will be dealt with more fully in Part Four, when we come to the general topic of adult learning and education.

What Change Is Possible in Adulthood?

Very little change is possible in a person's *basic* nature during adulthood (or even during middle to late childhood). One of the grand mistakes of human history has been to rely *too much* on changing people (including oneself) at this fundamental level. It has led to untold

19. E. Durkheim, *Moral Education* (New York: Free Press, 1961; originally 1925), pp. 119-20.
20. M. Apple, *Ideology and Curriculum*, 2nd ed. (London: Routledge and Kegan Paul, 1989), pp. 154-66.
21. Gregory Baum, *Religion and Alienation* (New York: Paulist Press, 1975), pp. 199-204.

atrocities through attempts to force people to change, and great expense and disillusionment as one educational program after another has been tried and has largely failed. In families, schools, and individual adult lives today it continues to be a source of great interpersonal friction and unnecessary disappointment. Furthermore, the fruitless attempt to change people at this basic level diverts attention and resources from more feasible avenues of change.

Most of the universal changes in adulthood noted earlier were not changes in people's basic nature. Rather, they were shifts in people's perspective and behavior due to a changing time frame, bodily aging, and age-related changes in circumstances. They did not involve people becoming substantially more or less selfish, for example, or secure (within themselves), or tolerant *in general*.

Of course, the distinction between people's "basic nature" and their "perspective and behavior" is not clear-cut. However, what I am proposing is that we distinguish broadly between what people value and do because of their nature or personality, and what they value and do because of their knowledge and circumstances. People don't have to change in their basic nature in order to achieve considerable advances in attitude, behavior, happiness, and well-being.

A distinction of this kind is what David Gauthier has in mind when he talks of people's moral "dispositions" and "policies," on the one hand, and their moral knowledge and actions, on the other. According to Gauthier, children's "spontaneous desire to please" others and their "sympathetic responses to the joys and sorrows of others" are formed at quite an early age. Similarly, the dispositions or virtues which comprise our moral character, such as courage or fairness, along with the "policy" of "treating others as objects of concern," are largely established (insofar as they are) by middle childhood, as a result of example, imitation, praise, reward, admonition, and "learn(ing) to value by being in a community of valuers."[22] The main task of moral *education*, then, as distinct from early moral *training*, is to teach people about the consequences of their actions. While there is not much that can be done to change basic dispositions, in the area of the *effects* of human action existing information "is sufficient to provide us with an awareness and an understanding far exceeding that which we actually employ (at present) in educating people about what they do" (p. 145. My parentheses). Gauthier gives an example of the problems created by our lack of awareness of what we do:

> The condition of Blacks in America or Natives in Canada is not primarily the effect of deliberate racism, although it is easy enough for racists to have their way. Rather, these conditions result from social policies which have not brought the resources of society effectively to bear on the transformation of the material and social environment . . . . And these social policies are not so much the policies of racists as the policies of the indifferent, of those whose moral sensitivity has not been directed to the real consequences of what they do. (p. 145)

Moral education is aimed, then, not at people who lack moral character or generous dispositions, but "at those who, possessing these characteristics, nevertheless fail to do as they ought because 'they do not know what they do'." Of course, such education will not necessarily be popular. "People do not always wish to know the consequences of their action, especially if that knowledge will oblige them to change their behavior at some inconvenience to themselves" (p. 146). But over time the imparting

22. D. Gauthier, "Moral Action and Moral Education," in *Moral Education: Interdisciplinary Approaches*, eds. C. Beck, B. Crittenden, and E. Sullivan (Toronto: University of Toronto Press, 1971), pp. 141-44.

of morally relevant information offers enormous potential for increasing the morality of people's behavior without any necessary change in basic dispositions (although specific dispositions — for example toward people of other races — may change substantially).

Another major way in which people's behavior and well-being can change is through changes in the context in which they live. If, as Apple maintains, individuals have difficulty behaving well in a faulty social structure, this problem can be alleviated by improvements in the society. (Also, individuals can change their *personal* environment to some extent, thus helping to provide the "enabling circumstances" they need, as we saw in Chapter 3.) Gauthier perhaps does not recognize sufficiently this aspect of the problem, placing too much emphasis on the power of knowledge. In Part 4 we will discuss at greater length the role of societal reconstruction in value change.

In conclusion, we should note that *some* change in basic personality characteristics is possible, even in difficult social and cultural circumstances. Perhaps Gauthier and Apple have taken unduly pessimistic positions in this respect. However, in view of the observed continuities in people's basic nature and values, the *emphasis* in adult values education must shift dramatically. Much more attention must be given to changes, for example, in knowledge and in the individual and social context of our lives which do not require basic personality change.

CHAPTER 9

Gender Differences in Values in Adulthood

Having looked at patterns of adult values in general, we turn now to a specific area which has been receiving increasing attention from psychologists and others, namely, gender differences in values. After a brief examination of phase and stage approaches to the area, I will focus on gender differences which tend to persist throughout life, taking up the question whether these differences could and should be reduced or even eliminated. I will argue that change is indeed possible and that, given the amount of harm which results from such differences, we should work toward a convergence of female and male values and related patterns of life.

Phase and Stage Differences Between the Sexes

Differences in the developmental patterns of women and men in our culture have been identified. While we must be wary (in the spirit of preceding chapters) of overstating the developmental differences between the genders, and the differences between age groups within a gender, the differences that exist have important practical implications.

Looking first at *phases* of development, Sheehy's account of sex differences in *Passages* is perhaps the most detailed. She notes, for example, that while for most women in their twenties the intimacy of marriage and child rearing is at the centre of their life and provides "completion," for most men of the same age marriage is a much less important aspect of life and is largely part of the background they need for pursuing individualistic goals (pp. 97 and 145). At the Catch-30 passage (age 28–32), many men change from wanting a mother figure to wanting a companion (but *not* a rival), while for many women, still grappling with child rearing, such a change in their husband's wishes comes too early (and too late) (pp. 202-207). At age thirty-five many married women do an "all-points survey," looking for ways to get more out of life, despite social conventions; for many married men, however, this comes at the worst possible time, since they are in a phase of wanting to reach the top of their career and also become a pillar of social respectability (pp. 44 and 169). In the forties transition, some men feel they have catching up to do in terms of family intimacy, whereas many women seek a different kind of catching up which may lead away from the home to some extent (pp. 44-45 and 425-27). In middle adulthood, women are more likely than men to feel superfluous due to the empty nest syndrome; while at retirement men are in greater danger than women of suffering a sudden loss of meaning in life (pp. 497-500).

In presenting this material on age-related differences I have added qualifiers such as "most," "many," and "some." Sheehy herself, as we saw in Chapter 6, vacillates between making universal statements — women in their mid-twenties do this, men in their mid-thirties experience that — and noting exceptions. If we are to use her insights, we must go beyond her text and assess the *extent* to which a particular gender difference occurs, and at a particular age level. Also we must consider to what degree patterns have changed in the twenty years or so since Sheehy's research was done.

Carol Gilligan has also written about differences between female and male value development, although more in terms of *stages* than phases (and with a focus on *moral* development). In *In a Different Voice*, referring to girls and women, she points to a "sequence of development" as follows:

- *First perspective:* caring for the self in order to ensure survival;
- *Transitional phase:* criticism of the first perspective as selfish;
- *Second perspective:* responsibility; caring for the dependent and unequal;
- *Transitional phase:* experience of disequilibrium due to problems arising from the exclusion of self;
- *Third perspective:* interdependence; differentiating self and other and caring for both.[1]

While the three perspectives occur in this sequence, the *rate* at which they unfold varies greatly from person to person and some women never reach the third perspective (or even the second).

In a sense, the three perspectives outlined by Gilligan are found in boys and men also, corresponding roughly to Kohlberg's pre-conventional, conventional, and post-conventional levels. Consistent sex differences in stages of

1. C. Gilligan, *In a Different Voice* (Cambridge, MA: Harvard University Press, 1982), p.73.

development have not been observed.[2] However, according to Gilligan, females and males differ in the *manner* in which they approach morality. Whereas males have justice as their goal and tend to pursue it as rugged individuals, females focus on care and seek to achieve it in a network of relationships.

In a recent book, *Making Connections*,[3] Gilligan has done some phase theorizing. She sees ages eleven and twelve as an especially critical period, when girls have a clear glimpse of the compromises contemporary society forces upon women, before they are plunged into the tensions of adolescence. Beginning in adolescence, females are required in our society to make major concessions "in order to survive or to appear good in the eyes of others (and thus sustain their protection)." These choices "often feel disruptive to women" and "are often at the expense of women's relationships with one another," but women frequently have no alternative (pp. 25-27), and as a result lose the insight into reality they had prior to this period:

> Although Laura, at sixteen, is more sophisticated in her thinking and at a more advanced level in Loevinger's scale of ego development than twelve-year-old Tanya, something is different in mid-adolescence. From listening to her responses . . . it appears that Laura does not have Tanya's clear way of speaking nor Tanya's knowledge of relationships — a knowledge that does not exclude herself. (p. 328)

In light of such observations, Gilligan is inclined to see her three-level developmental sequence as applicable only

2. C. Gilligan, J. V. Ward, and J. M. Taylor, *Mapping the Moral Domain* (Cambridge, MA: Harvard University Press, 1988), pp. 73, 82-83.
3. C. Gilligan, N. Lyons, and T. Hanmer, eds., *Making Connections: The Relational Worlds of Adolescent Girls at Emma Willard School* (Cambridge, MA: Harvard University Press, 1990).

to the later adolescent and adult period of women's lives, brought on by the distinctive challenges which begin in adolescence in our society (pp. 9-10). In her view, the strongly emerging insight of female children into the human (and in particular women's) condition is rudely interrupted in adolescence by pressure to conform to a male-dominated society, which requires a new set of choices and leads to a new sequence of development. Females who progressed well in childhood moral development may fare quite badly, at least for a period, in adolescence and beyond.

Stage theories such as Gilligan's, as we saw in Chapter 7, have the same potential as phase theories to stereotype particular age groups and, in the present case, a particular gender. We must consider carefully whether or not *all* females go through the stages and phases Gilligan outlines, and whether or not at least *some* males share similar experiences and changes. In *In a Different Voice* Gilligan speaks of a possible convergence of women and men in adulthood as each group achieves the insights and virtues of the other.[4] To what extent might the beginnings of such convergence be detected in childhood and adolescence? Indeed, some would say that today there is more convergence between females and males in childhood and adolescence than in adulthood: that our young people are leading the way toward reduced differentiation along gender lines. Nevertheless, it is clear that Gilligan has identified characteristics and struggles which, at the very least, are *more* typical of females than of males.

4. *In a Different Voice*, pp. 165-67.

Enduring Gender Differences in Attitudes, Outlook, and Life-Style

While, as we have seen, there are age- and stage-related gender differences in values, many of the differences between women and men are rather constant from adolescence (and earlier) to the end of life. In this section, I will review some of the lifelong differences which have been identified by psychologists and others.

As with developmental differences, the enduring differences between women and men have often been exaggerated: they are certainly there as an *average tendency*, but there are more exceptions than many theorists have suggested. The following account of differences, with quotations from the literature, reflects to some extent exaggerations in the field. Nevertheless, the average differences are indeed quite marked, and they help explain many of the difficulties women and men have in living their own lives and relating to each other.

While describing the following characteristics as "enduring," I don't wish to suggest that change is not possible. The differences are largely due to different circumstances, which could change. Even at present there are cases where, for example, a woman becomes more justice-oriented over time or a man becomes more interested in relationships. And let us hope that, in the future, as the harm done by present gender patterns becomes more widely understood, and as gender inequality is reduced, considerable change will often be achieved within a person's lifetime. These differences, then, are typically but not necessarily lifelong.

a. *Care versus Justice Orientation.* According to Gilligan (as we have seen) and Nel Noddings, women typically adopt a care perspective in ethics while men tend to make judgments on the basis of justice. Discussing modern moral philosophy, Noddings says that it has been distorted by the male focus on rationality and justice, to the neglect of the female emphasis on caring.

> . . . ethics has been discussed largely in the language of the father: in principles and propositions, in terms such as justification, fairness, justice. The mother's voice has been silent. Human caring and the memory of caring and being cared for . . . have not received attention except as outcomes of ethical behavior.[5]

Noddings doesn't deny that men can be caring. But the very title of her book, *Caring: A Feminine Approach to Ethics and Moral Education,* makes it clear that, in her view, women are typically more caring than men.

b. *Open-mindedness versus Narrowness and Inflexibility.* An aspect of Noddings's general position is that women are more open to concrete, intuitively understood, *actual* reality; while men tend to follow inflexible principles and rational procedures which blind them to important elements of experience. In Gilligan's terms, women are more open to knowledge which "comes not from detachment but from living in connection with themselves and with others, from being embedded in the conditions of life."[6] This position is developed further by Mary Field Belenky and others in *Women's Ways of Knowing,* where it is argued that women are in a distinctively strong position to cover the whole spectrum of types of knowledge: "reason *and* intuition *and* the expertise of others."[7] Women are distinctively open to the insight that "all

5. N. Noddings, *Caring: A Feminine Approach to Ethics and Moral Education* (Berkeley: University of California Press, 1984), p. 1.
6. *In a Different Voice,* p. 148.
7. M. F. Belenky, B. M. Clinchy, N. R. Goldberger, and J. M. Tarule, *Women's Ways of Knowing* (New York: Basic Books, 1986), p. 133.

knowledge is constructed" and "the knower is an intimate part of the known" (p. 137).

> Women become aware that questions and answers vary throughout history, across cultures, from discipline to discipline, and from individual to individual. . . .
>
> . . . Women tend not to rely as readily or as exclusively on hypothetico-deductive inquiry, which posits an answer (the hypothesis) prior to the data collection, as they do on examining basic assumptions and the conditions in which a problem is cast. (pp. 138-39)

Some men, of course, also have these insights; and many women do not. But women are more inclined to have them than men, who have been chiefly responsible for "the perception of science as absolute truth or as a procedure for obtaining objective facts" (p. 138). On the whole, the powerful ways of knowing "that women have cultivated and learned to value . . . have been neglected and denigrated by the dominant (male oriented) intellectual ethos of our time" (p. ix. Parentheses added).

c. *Connectedness versus Individualism.* Women usually value relationships highly, while men typically try to succeed as "rugged individuals." As Jean Baker Miller states:

> . . . women's sense of personhood is grounded in the motivation to make and enhance relatedness to others. We observe that women tend to find satisfaction, pleasure, effectiveness, and a sense of worth if they experience their life activities as arising from, and leading back into, a sense of connection with others. This view differs in its basic premises from most current (male oriented) psychological theories

> which tend to center on the development of a more separated sense of self.[8]

The difference between men and women in this respect is noted by Gilligan:

> Since masculinity is defined through separation while femininity is defined through attachment, male gender identity is threatened by intimacy while female gender identity is threatened by separation. Thus males tend to have difficulty with relationships, while females tend to have problems with individuation.[9]

Stephen Bergman, while arguing that modern psychology has exaggerated the difference between women and men in this area, nevertheless identifies sex differences with respect to relationships. He says that "for men as well as women, there is a primary desire for connection with others"; however, from about the age of three,

> . . . the boy is heavily pressured to disconnect, to achieve maleness . . . (there is) a break from *being in the process* with a person . . . it is not "separating from the mother" or "disconnecting from the mother," it's *a disconnecting from the very process of growth in relationship*, a learning about *turning away from the whole relational mode.*
>
> This turning-away-from means that the boy never really learns *how* to do it . . . .[10]

8. J. B. Miller, "What Do We Mean By Relationships?", *Work in Progress*, No. 22 (1986), The Stone Center, Wellesley College, Wellesley, MA, p. 1. Parentheses added.
9. *In a Different Voice*, p. 8.
10. S. Bergman, "Men's Psychological Development: A Relational Perspective," *Work in Progress*, No. 48 (1991), The Stone Center, Wellesley College, Wellesley, MA, pp. 3-4.

d. *Co-operation and Compromise versus Competition and Confrontation.* According to Miller:

> Another important aspect of women's psychology is their greater recognition of the essential cooperative nature of human existence . . . women in families are constantly trying to work out some sort of cooperative system that attends to each person's needs. Their task is greatly impeded by the unequal premise on which our families are based, but it has been women who have *practiced* trying.[11]

In order to achieve co-operation, especially under conditions of unequal power, women must constantly engage in and encourage compromise. Men, by contrast, tend to see situations in terms of competing interests and winners and losers; and instead of making compromises they exercise their power, either to achieve advantage for themselves or to impose unilaterally a "just solution."

While women are less confrontational, it should be noted that they don't necessarily shy away from conflict: indeed they see it as essential. As Bergman notes, women see the possibility and necessity of "staying connected through conflict." By contrast, "men often wind up being deadly afraid of conflict — perhaps more so than women," because sustained interpersonal conflict involves being in a close relationship, which so many men dread.[12]

e. *Awareness of Weakness versus Sense of Strength.* Miller points out that while feelings of weakness, vulnerability, and helplessness may be pathological when they occur in an extreme form, a degree of awareness of one's weaknesses is important for daily living. She comments:

11. J. B. Miller, *Toward a New Psychology of Women*, 2nd ed. (Boston: Beacon Press, 1986), p. 41.
12. "Men's Psychological Development," p. 5.

> In Western society men are encouraged to dread, abhor, or deny feeling weak or helpless, whereas women are encouraged to cultivate this state of being.[13]

Men often rely on women to solve their problems, because they can't themselves acknowledge them. However, because of the psychological and political dynamic of the situation, the contribution of women often can't be admitted, even by themselves. Miller gives an example of a man who "harbored the seemingly contradictory wish that his wife would somehow solve everything for him with such magic and dispatch that he would never be aware of his weakness at all." When his wife "did not instantly accomplish this feat for him," he was angry at her because of the attention her attempt had brought to his weakness. If she had been clever enough, he would not have had to notice either his problem or his wife's solution of it! (p. 33).

f. *Emotionality versus Non-Emotionality*. According to Miller, most women "have a much greater sense of the emotional components of all human activity than most men." Women believe that "events are important and satisfying only if they occur within the context of emotional relatedness." In our male-dominated culture, emotionality has not been valued: it has been seen as an impediment to understanding and action (pp. 38-39). However, because of their subordinate position, women have developed a deep interest in emotions, having been compelled "to be attuned to the vicissitudes of mood, pleasure, and displeasure of the dominant group." Furthermore, "women have been so encouraged to concentrate on the emotions and reactions of others that they have been diverted from examining and expressing

13. *Toward a New Psychology of Women*, p. 29.

their emotions" (p. 39). We have the paradox, then, that women, who are so interested in feelings, often don't recognize why or even when they themselves have feelings such as anger or depression.

g. *Gentleness versus Aggression*. There is a distinctive female style of gentleness and a common male style of aggressiveness or violence. Gilligan reports a study of the use of images of violence in stories written by men and women: of eighty-eight men, 51 percent wrote at least one story containing violent images, in comparison to 20 percent of fifty women in a comparable group; and no woman wrote more than one story in which violence appeared.[14] She goes on to cite findings presented by Freud in his 1930 book *Civilization and Its Discontents*:

> . . . women appear as the exception to the rule of relationships, by demonstrating a love not admixed with anger, a love arising . . . from a feeling of connection, a primary bond between other and self. But this love of the mother cannot, Freud says, be shared by the son, who would thus "make himself dependent in a most dangerous way . . . ." (pp. 46-47)
>
> . . . Throughout Freud's work women remain the exception to his portrayal of relationships, and they sound a continuing theme, of an experience of love which . . . does not appear to have separation and aggression at its base. (p. 47)

It should be noted that Gilligan does not link this non-aggressive love to weakness. She sees it as compatible with the characteristic female state of "interdependence" (p. 47), in which women show determination and courage in balancing concern for others and concern for self. We

14. *In a Different Voice*, p. 41.

may draw a parallel here with the Taoist notion of gentleness which, while it is the opposite of a ruthless, exploitative approach to life, does not imply weakness or indecisiveness: it involves a careful "going with the flow," acting firmly but with kindness and a due sense of what is possible and needed.

h. *Giving versus Doing*. In Miller's words:

> Women constantly confront themselves with questions about giving. Am I giving enough? Can I give enough? Why don't I give enough? They frequently have deep fears about what this must mean about them. They are upset if they feel they are not givers. . . .
>
> By contrast, the question of whether he is a giver or giving enough does not enter a man's self-image. Few men feel that giving is a primary issue in their struggles for identity. They are concerned much more about "doing." . . . In fact, to be seen as too much of a giver is something of a detraction, implying that one is a little too soft, a bit of a patsy.[15]

Both women and men, then, are locked into their respective roles of giving and doing by the culture in which they live. Miller notes that "many men clearly long to give of themselves," but they can do so "only *after* they have fulfilled the primary requirements of manhood."[16]

15. *Toward a New Psychology of Women*, p. 50.
16. *Ibid.*, p. 50.

Harm Resulting from Sex Differences

Many writers have noted the harm to women caused by lack of appreciation of their distinctive strengths. Gilligan in *In A Different Voice* documents how women have been judged to have an inferior morality because it differs from the dominant, male-oriented morality. Instead of being celebrated for their emphasis on care, co-operation, emotionality, and gentleness, women have been viewed and treated as inferior beings, lacking in rationality, determination, moral fibre, and clarity of moral vision. Instead of being praised for their cultivation of family and friendship ties, they have been dismissed as "mired in relationships." Instead of being seen as appropriately flexible, they have been regarded as lacking in principle.

The time has come, of course, to reject strenuously this assessment of women's morality. Despite the achievements of modern Western culture, the harm done by "warrior-king" morality indicates that a major shift toward the womanly virtues is in order. As we saw earlier, Gilligan has proposed a convergence in the morality of women and men: instead of one gender looking down their noses at the morality of the other, there should be an acceptance and pooling of each other's insights and virtues.

In this section, however, I wish to focus not so much on prejudice and discrimination between the sexes as on the harm resulting from gender differences. I will argue that *both* sexes suffer greatly as a result of the current pattern of sex-differentiated values and ways of life.

Gilligan has noted the problems created for women by excessive self-sacrifice, by "their own exclusion of themselves."[17] Self-sacrificing women often suffer from a sense of vulnerability, a poor self-concept, indecisiveness,

17. *In A Different Voice*, p. 149.

and lack of self-confidence (pp. 64-68, 87-95). She proposes a shift from self-sacrifice to "interdependence," an approach in which one attempts "to be responsible to (oneself) as well as to others and thus to reconcile the disparity between hurt and care" (p. 82. Parentheses added).

Miller has elaborated comprehensively and in detail how women suffer as a result of their distinctive pattern of values. She emphasizes the benefits of women's propensity for caring, connectedness, co-operation, humility, emotionality, and so forth. But she sees each of these virtues as being "two-sided." While they are "sources of strength and the bases of a more advanced form of living," nevertheless, "in a situation of inequality and powerlessness, these characteristics can lead to subservience and to complex psychological problems."[18] Women's strengths are also weaknesses, because they involve serious neglect and even lack of awareness of women's own needs. As a result many women end up angry, depressed, demoralized, and exhausted.

Men also suffer from the present female–male dichotomy in personal characteristics and patterns of life. While they are the dominant group, they are largely cut off from many capacities, experiences, and relationships essential to the good life. They are much worse off than they would be if they were in an equal relationship with women and shared their virtues. It is disastrous for men that they are afraid to be caring, are narrow-minded, have difficulty being flexible and compromising, fear close and equal relationships with women, have trouble admitting their weaknesses, lack emotionality, and so on. The males in Miller's cases are often pathetic figures: for example, the man who cannot acknowledge his severe stress symptoms, or admit his wife's key role in helping him

18. *Toward a New Psychology of Women*, p. 27.

deal with them; and the man who cannot consider reducing his pay or hours of work to foster and enjoy his children's development and to enable his wife to maintain her work outside the home, but who nevertheless is filled with dread and despair at the thought of losing his family (pp. 38ff. and 68ff.).

Bergman is eloquent in describing the difficulties encountered by men as a result of their distinctive way of life. Concentrating especially on men's lack of capacity for close relationships, he says:

> As with women, the seeds of misery in men's lives are planted in disconnection with others, in isolation, violation and dominance, and in relationships which are not mutually empowering. To participate in relationships which are not mutual is a source of sadness and rage, which, even in the dominant gender, can lead over a period of time to withdrawal, stagnation, and depression, and, characteristically, insecurity, aggression, and violence.[19]

While men are at ease with each other at a superficial level, even male–male relationships are adversely affected by the competitive, non-mutual ethos of the dominant culture.

> In a patriarchy, men may *also* be victims. Hierarchy means that there's always someone *more* successful and *more* powerful, and men are haunted by failure. The biggest winners are potentially the biggest losers. In a power-*over* model, it isn't safe to take an authentic, vulnerable, relational stance.[20]

19. "Men's Psychological Development," p. 4.
20. *Ibid.*, p. 7.

Men also suffer as a result of the constraints placed on *women's* development in our culture. If women were allowed to pursue their interests and develop their capacities more fully, they would be more interesting partners. If they were able to be more openly critical of men's lives, they could give more assistance to men in their attempts to live well. If they were permitted to be stronger, they could give more support to men. If they earned more, they could reduce the pressure on men to be such a major source of financial security.

Apart from problems inherent in the respective gender characteristics, the mere fact that women and men are so *different* from each other creates severe difficulties. While there are times when difference "adds spice to life," on the whole the great gulf between the sexes means that full and satisfying relationships between women and men are difficult to attain. Constant incompatibility arises because of differences in interests, tastes, styles, pleasures, ambitions, and so on. Even in the area where — for many men — the chief object in relating to women lies, namely sexuality, we often have the irony that an intimate, sensual experience is sought between two people who, because of their upbringing, don't understand or appreciate each other, have difficulty communicating with each other, and have different sexual ideals and pleasures.

Toward Female–Male Convergence

In my view, it is clear from the foregoing that we should move as quickly as possible toward a world in which differences in values and other personal characteristics are not gender related. Both women and men should typically have the full range of what are currently feminine and masculine virtues. Gender linked anatomical and physiological characteristics and biological functions should not, wholly or partly, determine one's personality or way of life. This, of course, would require gender equality, economically, politically, occupationally, and so on; but that too is desirable, even from men's point of view. As we have seen, inequality along gender lines does no one any good, all things considered.

Is it possible for women and men to have what are currently each other's virtues? Gilligan, Miller, Bergman, and others seem to allow for this. Gilligan, as we have seen, speaks of "convergence." Miller stresses again and again that current gender patterns are due to political, economic, and cultural (rather than biological) factors, and accordingly could in principle be changed. For example, she says:

> Subordinates . . . become highly attuned to the dominants, able to predict reactions to pleasure and displeasure. Here, I think, is where the long history of "feminine intuition" and "feminine wiles" begins. It seems clear that these "mysterious" gifts are in fact skills, developed through long practice in reading many signals, both verbal and non-verbal.[21]

Elsewhere, Miller maintains that men, too, are products of our culture. With respect to the men in two of her examples she states:

> Neither Judy's nor Edith's husband wanted to hurt or deprive anyone. This was, in fact, one reason why they reacted so negatively when their wives first raised the issue of deprivation. It made them feel cruel when they never intended to be. This issue rests on a deeper point, however: In order to pursue their *prescribed male identity,* they had learned to close off large areas of their sensibilities;

21. *Toward a New Psychology of Women,* p. 10.

one area is precisely that of responsiveness to the needs of others. (p. 69. Italics added.)

Bergman also ties the differences between females and males to cultural factors. He claims that male and female development is quite similar "until about the age of three," at which time "everything in the culture" forces disconnection of the boy from his mother "in the name of 'growth'."[22] All involved — child, mother, father, other relatives, teachers, friends — think the boy will have difficulty surviving as a boy in our culture unless he strikes out on his own; and so they all contribute to his movement away from relationships.

A convergence in female and male characteristics, then, seems possible. But what, precisely, is the goal we should be aiming at? Should there be an equal pooling of virtues, or should those of one sex predominate?

I believe that both women *and* men have many virtues to contribute; but some of the writers we have been discussing seem to see the female approach to life as superior. For example, as we saw earlier, in *Women's Ways of Knowing,* Belenky et al. claim that women's openness to reason *and* intuition *and* the expertise of others places them in a distinctively strong position to pursue knowledge. And Miller in *Toward a New Psychology for Women* offers a very positive view of women's way of life (and a largely negative view of men's), and suggests that men's way may have been "a vast, unnecessary detour" whereas we have "already available" in women's way "the basis for what seem the absolutely essential next steps in Western history if we are to survive."[23] Elsewhere she says: "This psychic starting point (women's) contains the possibilities for an entirely different (and more advanced) approach to living and functioning — very different, that

22. "Men's Psychological Development," p. 4.
23. *Toward a New Psychology of Women,* p. 88.

is, from the approach fostered by the dominant (i.e. male oriented) culture" (p. 83. First and third parentheses added).

While it is clearly essential to argue at length for women's strengths, given the way they have been systematically downgraded, I believe it is a mistake to maintain that women have *in general* better values than men (or vice versa). This is like claiming that Muslims are in general better than Christians or that the French are in general superior to the English. For one thing it is extremely difficult to justify such notions, given the range of life areas in question; but just as importantly, such claims establish a negative dynamic within which it is difficult for the two groups to grow, whether separately or together. In the case of women and men, we need a basic assumption that both genders are capable of roughly equal virtue — and, I would say, the same virtues — and a determination to *work together* to achieve a better *human* way of life. Such mutual goodwill and co-operation is especially necessary given the way women's and men's lives are so intertwined (and must be increasingly in the future); and given the current disparity in power, and the need not to alienate men but rather enlist their aid in the changes. Miller and others have shown in such detail how women take on the perceptions of themselves held by men and the patterns of behavior expected by men; it would be ironic, then, for women to attempt to build a new way of life largely out of relation with men. We must assume that men have as many insights as women into how to live the good life, that the distinctive insights of each gender can usefully be pooled, that there is much in common to be celebrated, and that a great many additional insights can be attained in the future by working together in a mutually accepting, relational process.

The virtues of men are often difficult to see. However, I believe this is because they are so much part of our culture's accepted way of doing things that we don't realize what they contribute or where we would be without them. General broadsides against modern scientific, technological, bureaucratic society have their place. Contemporary Western culture certainly has many weaknesses. But science, technology, and bureaucracy have brought many benefits to both women and men; what is needed is not their abolition but the development of new forms of them which combine their present strengths with new positive elements (suggested in large measure by women's ways of knowing and living).

But are we ready for a convergence of the distinctively female and male? In many ways we are not, either politically or psychologically. It is still "a man's world," and the pressure both women and men experience to live out a distinctive role remains strong. In this climate, it is natural for both genders to seek comfort, support, and insight from their own kind (we now have a burgeoning "men's movement"). However, whatever stop-gap measures we adopt in the short-term, I believe it is essential to see as the long-term goal a world in which one's gender is largely irrelevant, a world in which we think of *human* development rather than female or male development.

Of course, women will always have a distinctive role in that only they can bear children. Further, child bearing typically gives a woman an attachment to her child that men often do not share. However, once again the *ideal* is to reach a point where men have equal attachment to their children and similar qualities of care, gentleness, flexibility, and so on, which make for good "mothering." The experience of gestation and giving birth will always be unique to women. But we must assume that, eventually, as many men as women *could* attain the attachments and qualities needed for parenting. If we don't, we will be putting a major impediment in the way of the feminization of men.

What about sexuality? Could that survive the convergence of women and men? Obviously it could. Already we see how homosexual couples (female and male) can have emotional, "magical," physically and spiritually exciting relationships. It would be absurd to suggest that women and men, because they had too many interests in common and too many similarities of taste and style, could not have strongly sexual relationships. On the contrary, it is likely that such couples would experience much more sexual pleasure and "magic" than is usual among heterosexual partners at present.

Many of the writers on gender differences seem rather pessimistic about the possibilities for female–male convergence. While history and personal experience are on their side, I think there is room for optimism. On the one hand, the opportunities for the dissemination of new ideas in the world are rapidly growing. And on the other hand, in the matter of gender differences and bias I believe that ideas and information could have a major impact. The notions we have been discussing in this chapter — that women have many strengths hitherto unacknowledged by men or even by themselves; that men have many limitations and stand in need of feminine virtues; that both women *and* men suffer enormously as a result of present gender patterns; and that the origins of these patterns are cultural rather than biological — are new to most people, and awareness of them through word of mouth, the mass media, popular books, formal education, and so on could lead to extensive changes.

Bergman quotes a man at one of his workshops as saying: "Men want relationship, sure, but the bottom line is we don't want to give up our power to get it."[24] Similarly, Miller states that once a man is established in his way of life it is hard for him "to give up the push

24. "Men's Psychological Development," p. 10.

toward aggression and the belief in its necessity."[25] But I think these views reveal undue pessimism about human nature. Men are people too; can they really be so foolish as to stick obstinately to their ways, unaffected by knowledge of how their aggression and unequal power spoil their lives and those of their loved ones? I don't wish to be naive about the efficacy of education or the power of ideas by themselves to bring about change. Many supplementary forces will be necessary: the direct influence and pressure of women, institutional changes, laws against violence, equity laws, strict law enforcement, social movements of various kinds. But clear and comprehensive discussion of the issues in various settings could do much to reduce the harm resulting from current gender patterns.

25. *Toward a New Psychology of Women*, p. 87.

Part Three:

The Importance of Values In Adulthood

In Part One it was claimed that values promote well-being or the good life. Part Three illustrates in more detail how this happens. It is shown (in Chapter 10) how a goal-oriented approach to values enables us to establish priorities in life, set limits, achieve optimal integration, and "make the most of life" in difficult circumstances. More specifically, it is shown (in Chapter 11) how a sound values approach can help us achieve friendship, freedom from undue stress, interesting work, health, an aesthetic way of life, and good family relationships. Chapter 11 is unusual in format. While it serves to demonstrate the fruitfulness of a values approach to life problems, it has been designed also for use in group discussion. Adult educators are encouraged to experiment with it in such a context.

CHAPTER 10

The Role of Values in Adult Life

The *general* role values play in our lives is clear from Part One. Values keep us "on course" in the pursuit of well-being, for ourselves and others. Basic values define that well-being, and intermediate-range and specific values indicate in more detail how to pursue it. Values give "direction" to our lives. This direction is not necessarily externally imposed, nor is it permanently fixed: we constantly modify our values as our interests and life circumstances shift and as our understanding of reality changes. However, at any given time our values tell us how to live the good life.

We must now look at what this means in more practical terms. How exactly do values enhance the well-being of humans, and in particular of adults? In this chapter I will describe the role of values in helping us set priorities, recognize limits, achieve integration, and "make the most of life." Finally, in the last section, I will try to counter the objection that there are negative side effects of a values-oriented approach to life which outweigh the benefits.

Establishing Priorities

To begin with, values help us achieve well-being by enabling us to set priorities. With a well-developed value system we can distinguish between more and less important activities: what we should spend more and less time and resources on, what we should do sooner, what we *must* do but can delay for a while, and what we can postpone and if necessary omit completely.

Establishing priorities in life is of crucial importance since some activities promote well-being more than others and so must be given priority in order to maximize well-being. For example, our family life, in both the short- and long-term, may be of great significance to us and to other family members. If we recognize this fact and take steps to give it priority, we will be able to avoid having it crowded out by other commitments — at work, in the community, with non-family friends — which we take on without seeing the consequences. Again, having a job we enjoy is a great bonus during the whole of our working life. If we see this value and rearrange our life so we can — perhaps after a delay — get into an interesting job, the life-time benefits will be considerable. Of course, anything can happen: we may be hit by a bus before we can enjoy our carefully chosen career. But for most people, in reasonably stable circumstances, such planning is clearly worthwhile.

As well as being "objectively" unwise, failure to prioritize can have a number of unfortunate "subjective" consequences such as worry, indecision, frustration, and boredom. If we don't figure out at least roughly what is more and less important in life, we will often be upset (and will upset others) by our indecision. Then, having made certain choices and commitments, we may worry that there are crucial values we are neglecting; and as time passes, and it becomes clear that this is so, we will become even more aggravated and worried insofar as we can't do anything about it. Further, a major source of frustration and boredom in life arises from finding ourselves doing endless tasks (for example, excessive and uninteresting committee work and "administrivia") which we *could* have avoided, at least to a degree, if we had had a clearer sense of what is important. Of course, some boring, stressful activity is necessary in life; but it should be avoided where possible. The irony is that some of the tasks we dislike but take on unthinkingly would be enjoyed by other people, whom we effectively prevent from having access to them.

Of course, the activity of developing priorities can itself be a source of frustration. It involves gaining an overview of our lives (including the limitations and eventual final limit of life) which we may find disturbing; and it involves setting aside other interesting activities and engaging in systematic thought and planning which we may not enjoy. However, setting priorities will *on balance and in the long-run* reduce frustration and boredom and increase well-being.

Priorities are necessary because it is often not clear beforehand how much we will be able to get done. If we have priorities, we will be able to make provision for the more important things first and then fit in as many less important things as possible. As it becomes apparent that some of the latter cannot be done *at all*, we can take comfort in the fact that no great harm has been done because they are in fact of lesser importance. Also, where something of great importance comes up unexpectedly, we can quickly turn our attention to it because most of the more significant matters have been attended to, and less significant matters (which we have already identified) can be set aside temporarily or even permanently. For example, if there is a sudden death in our family we can focus on it fully, whereas if other key matters have not been taken care of, we may be hopelessly torn between conflicting demands.

It should be recognized that much of this prioritizing takes place automatically and naturally. It doesn't require that we be unusually introspective and self-conscious, and spend half our day drawing up lists of priorities and adding and subtracting various items. However, we do spend much of our day making choices, whether consciously or not: even to continue what we are doing requires some kind of resolve not to do something else. We are by nature choosing beings, and if we did not have direction and priorities we would not really have values at all. Prioritizing is actually just a matter of giving expression to our values, of taking our values seriously. What could it mean to say we had certain values if we didn't make choices designed to attain them? Even if we are often unconscious of our prioritizing and choosing, then, a well-developed value system is still needed to give appropriate direction to this process.

We might note in closing this section that the priorities in values I have been talking about are not the same as a "hierarchy" of values of the kind hypothesized by some theologians, philosophers, and psychologists. I don't believe there are broad categories of values (for example, social relationships, reflection, and "self-actualization") which are in general "above" or "superior" to others (for example, security, pleasure, material needs). My point, rather, is that certain *activities* must be given priority because they contribute to a high degree to people's *overall* well-being.

Setting Limits

Establishing priorities requires giving *prior* place, in emphasis and often in sequence, to some activities over others. Setting limits, on the other hand, involves accepting that there are some things we will not be able to do *at all*. We may support the idea of someone else doing them, and even arrange (where possible) for that to happen; but we frankly admit that *we* cannot do them.

Setting limits relates to values in two ways. On the one hand, certain goals are excluded from our value system because we simply can't do them, for example, become a professional opera singer or basketball player when we *clearly* do not have the necessary talent. In such cases, we really have no choice, but it is nevertheless important to recognize this fact on a continuing basis. On the other hand, many activities are excluded not because we couldn't do them but because, all things considered, they are not sufficiently worthwhile (for us). We "cannot" do them in the sense that we cannot fit them in. For example, I may be capable of becoming a politician or a union organizer but decide that, given the cost in terms of other important goals (family, career, social life, health, and so on) it is something I *should* not value (for myself).

Recognizing limits may involve reducing certain goals rather than eliminating them completely. For example, a person who wanted to be "a great success" both as a parent and in some career outside the home might choose more limited aims in both areas. (But how, our guilt feelings will say, can we settle for being a *moderate* success in parenting?) Or a union leader who wanted to be popular with the workers *and* management, but who lacks the time or talent to be both, might concentrate on the workers and aim at simply a reputation for reliability with management. The need, then, will be to overcome the sense of being a failure because we have lowered our sights; and to see that, overall, we are likely to achieve more than we would have if we had attempted to ignore our limitations.

In many cases, it is appropriate to avoid certain activities and situations completely. For example, a married couple who have reason to believe they couldn't cope with child rearing may decide not to have children. And people who find that remaining in a particular community is very important for their well-being may turn down offers of job promotion which would require them to move to another part of the country. The need, here, will be to see such avoidance behavior in a positive light; not as a sign of inadequacy, failure, cowardice, or lack of responsibility, but rather as a morally sound, courageous response to a complex situation.

Accepting that there are limits to what we can and should do is extremely important, but it is not handled well in contemporary society. It is remarkable the extent to which people plan to do things, or *feel guilty that they are not doing things,* which on careful consideration they would see they *should* not do, given their other value commitments. There is present in Western culture an ideology of "rising to every challenge" and a corresponding sense of guilt about not doing so. And this ideology, while appearing to be laudable, in fact saps our strength to do more important things. For if we try to do too much at once, we often end up doing nothing well; and if we are stressed because we are trying to do too much or guilty because there are some things we aren't doing, our general capacity to do good will be reduced.

Giving up "worthwhile" activities and turning down new "opportunities" is perhaps one of the most difficult things in life for people in certain sectors of society. Among those who are parents and/or are otherwise employed in a somewhat open-ended occupation, one of the most common complaints one hears is they are "too busy" to the point of virtual breakdown or almost perpetual joylessness. It is my contention that many of these people could increase their well-being, and the well-being of those around them, by being more selective in their commitments. In order to do so, however, they will have to develop a different perspective on their situation and also receive support from people around them. They will have to remind themselves (and be reminded) constantly of the extent of the harm that results from having too much to do, and the ways in which their lives could be enhanced by a more selective approach. And all this will have to take place against the background of a continually developing system of values which enables them to be selective.

Of course, it is often difficult to assess exactly how much we can do and accordingly how much we should take on. But we should constantly *attempt* this kind of assessment, rather than simply rising to every challenge that comes along. We should learn to say "no" and in good conscience. We will make mistakes, deleting some things we should not have; but *on balance* we will better promote the good life, for ourselves and others.

Achieving Integration

Developing a value system of the kind described in Part One helps ensure that we achieve a more integrated life. Basic goals are identified, related to each other, and linked to more specific values and to the whole set of experiences and activities which together promote the good life.

The relationship between values and integration is one of mutual support. Having a well worked out value system can make our life more integrated; and in certain respects the integration of our life is an important *means* to the more effective attainment of values. Sometimes *too much* significance has been attached to integration: it has been pursued as an absolute, an end in itself. As we saw in Chapter 3, there is a time for integration and a time for striking out in new directions. However, integration is valuable for several reasons.

To begin with, integration makes possible what Buckminster Fuller has called "synergy," literally, "working together." On the one hand, a number of goals may be pursued through the one activity (sometimes called "killing several birds with one stone"). For example, we may find an occupation which, as well as bringing in enough money, keeps us physically fit and enables us to be well-informed about a number of interesting areas. Or a relationship may not only meet our friendship needs but also lead to personal development (so-called "mentor" relationships are of this kind). On the other hand, synergy may take the form of achieving a single goal through the working together of several different activities. For example, our health may be maintained through a combination of exercise, appropriate diet, and certain life-style elements; or a couple's relationship may be helped through frank discussions, a change in job commitments, a broadening of the range of things they do together, and so on.

A degree of integration is also necessary to make possible the better *timing* of life events. This is important for several reasons. For example, the same activity (for example, changing jobs) can be a success or disaster depending on when it is done. Again, an excessive "bunching" of activities can transform a potentially manageable situation into one in which we cannot cope. Further, timing largely determines whether our activities build on each other or cancel each other out. However, without an integrated view of one's life it will be impossible to decide just when particular activities should occur.

An integrated understanding of life can also help give us a fuller sense of meaning in life. The mere fact that an activity or event fits into an overall pattern can give it meaning: we can then see it as "natural," "to be expected," or "the way things are." Beyond simply seeing a pattern in things, integration can give meaning because we see the purpose of particular activities: we see in detail how they contribute to other worthwhile aspects of our life. In this way, otherwise onerous tasks may become acceptable and even fulfilling.

Some writers on religion in recent years have recognized the role of values in contributing to an integrated world view or "faith" (in a broad sense). Wilfred Cantwell Smith, for example, has argued that what people embrace in their religion is not merely a set of beliefs but rather a total way of life, including everything one considers important in life. James Fowler summarizes Smith's position as follows: "Faith . . . is not a separate dimension of life, a compartmentalized speciality. Faith is an orientation of the total person, giving purpose and goal to one's hopes and strivings, thoughts and actions."[1] The point of faith inquiry, according to Fowler, is "to help us reflect on the centers of value and power that sustain our lives." The pattern of our faith consists in "the persons, causes, and institutions we really love and trust, the images of good and evil, of possibility and probability to which we are committed."[2] While I don't wish to use the word "faith" here because of its traditional religious connotations, I would agree that the kind of integrated approach these writers are speaking about, including a system of values along with other elements, is necessary to give life direction and meaning.

Making the Most of Things

Values are important in helping us find elements of good in situations which to other people might seem rather bleak. Our value system has often been seen in negative terms, as a basis for judgment and exclusion. But it can be viewed positively, as enabling us to be optimistic about life, to be aware of sources of well-being which we might otherwise overlook. It can make possible an enduring *joie de vivre.*

1. J. Fowler, *Stages of Faith* (San Francisco: Harper and Row, 1981), p. 14.
2. *Ibid.*, p. 4.

Accepting bleak situations is an important moral and spiritual virtue, much celebrated in both Eastern and Western religions. However, even when one is supposed to accept suffering "for the glory of God" or because "it is God's will," supplementary values are usually offered such as acquiring wisdom, or being "refined by fire," or being "rewarded in the next life." For the great majority of both religious and non-religious people, adopting an attitude of acceptance in a situation requires that we see some good in it *beyond* acceptance for its own sake. For this, we need a value system.

A value system can help us deal with adversity in two main ways. In the first place, as we have noted, it can often enable us to see good in a situation which has problematic features. Secondly, however, it can prepare us for adversity by steering us toward *a way of life* which is relatively well able to cope with setbacks. For example, if our values have led us to develop close community ties, we may be in a better position to survive losing a close friend or family member. Or if we have developed a wide range of sources of enjoyment, we may be better able to deal with being deprived of some of them because of poverty, physical handicap, or some other change in life circumstances. Generally speaking, if we don't put "too many eggs in one basket" — if not too many aspects of our way of life are related to one object, person, activity, or source of satisfaction — we will be less vulnerable. This may be seen, perhaps, as a qualification of the claim made earlier that our way of life should be integrated. However, the point is that our life, though integrated, should also be diversified: it shouldn't be integrated around a single focus. And we need a value system which helps work out the details of such a way of life.

No way of life is completely impervious to tragedy. Misfortune can wreak havoc in almost any way of life, and we are probably all vulnerable, no matter how many precautions we take. However, it would seem there is *something* in the promise held out by philosophy and religion through the millennia that they will enable us to rise, at least to a degree, above adversity. In my view, this promise is delivered in large measure through an adequate set of values.

Direction versus Spontaneity

What I've been proposing in this chapter — indeed, in this book — is that adult life must have a considerable degree of "direction" if we are to achieve well-being for ourselves and others. The direction, as noted before, need not be externally imposed or unchangeable; but without it, the good life won't be possible since the basic goals of life simply won't be attained.

We find widespread today, however, what might be called an "ideology of spontaneity," with extensive roots in Western literature, philosophy, and, more recently, social science. In part, perhaps, it has arisen as a legitimate reaction to excessively authoritarian and rigid traditions and institutions; but whatever its origins, it stands in contrast to the approach I have outlined. Against the relatively "directed" way of life I have proposed, the ideology of spontaneity would bring objections and arguments such as these:

- Intuition is the safest guide to living: general formulations of values and principles prevent us from seeing clearly.
- If we pursue happiness in a deliberate and systematic way it eludes us. The more we think and plan how to achieve beauty, fulfilment, love, and pleasure, the less we in fact achieve them.
- To approach issues using "value systems," "guidelines," and "life perspectives" is far too calculating and constraining. Spontaneity is much more attractive:

thoughtful, self-conscious people are awkward and boring.

In responding to these points, it is important to agree immediately that we should not weigh values every moment of the day. It is often necessary to move back and forth between thinking about how to do something and being absorbed in doing it. If we are always thinking about how to achieve happiness, for example, we will rarely be happy. Further, our approach to life should not be unduly cognitive: we must employ other sources of direction as well (as we saw in Chapters 2 and 3) such as intuition, feelings, and social contact. The values "direction" I am advocating comes only partly from the mind. At their very foundation, and throughout the "system," values are affective as well as cognitive; and in particular the body should influence the mind as much as the mind guides the body.

Having made these qualifications, however, we must nevertheless reject spontaneity as an *absolute* value or as *the* means to achieve life's values. To some extent humans do prize freedom for its own sake; but in attempting to attain our many values, we cannot afford to rely simply on free, spontaneous action. The complexity of life's decisions requires that we pursue a comprehensive set of values which takes account of the whole range of our needs. Each situation is different, and so value systems must be applied flexibly and be constantly open to change. But without principles and interconnected ideas we would get lost in the concrete details of each situation.

The argument from the attractiveness of spontaneity must also be rejected. People who are guided by values can be attractive, too, in their own way: think of the lives of historic teachers such as the Buddha, Socrates, Jesus. And actions based on countless hours of careful preparation can also be admired and enjoyed: consider the performances of great poets, musicians, dancers, actors.

Indeed, people who try to live completely spontaneously, without the "wisdom of the ages" or systematic reflection and preparation, often make such mistakes and end up in such despair that much of the beauty of their spontaneous life is lost.

To repeat, there is much to be learned from the ideology of spontaneity. Approaches to values in the modern era have often placed too much emphasis on principles and "rationality" and not enough on intuition, feeling, and flexibility. However, there is need for a "third alternative" which combines both structure and spontaneity. And in establishing this alternative, carefully articulated values play a crucial role.

CHAPTER 11

Applying a Values Approach to Adult Problems

(Sample Study Units)

In Chapter 10 I made a general case for the importance of values in adult life. But words are cheap, and it is easy to rationalize things which are not in fact worthwhile. In this chapter I wish to illustrate my position more concretely by showing the fruitfulness of a values approach to specific issues which adults face.

Illustrations *on paper* can also have an exaggerated plausibility, however. Accordingly, I have set out these examples so they can be used as discussion materials with adult groups. I have myself tried them in roughly this form with adults and adolescents and they have worked well. I commend them for use in adult groups, both to give assistance to people in living the good life and to help show the possibilities of values learning in adulthood. These, of course, are just a selection: there are literally hundreds of values topics which could usefully be considered by adults.

VALUES AND FRIENDSHIP

Idea for Discussion: To some extent friendship just "happens." We simply like certain people and want to spend time with them. However, **friendship fulfils certain values in our lives and so should be deliberately cultivated.** Values served by friends include the following:

- to keep us company
- to help us when things go wrong
- to share feelings
- to give us enjoyment and satisfaction
- to listen to us
- to help us learn about ourselves
- to help us learn about the world
- to give meaning to our life
- to help protect us against common enemies
- to help us do things we couldn't do alone

[*Discussion*: Do friends in fact serve these values? Can you think of examples? Do the rewards of friendship justify the time and resources expended and the quarrels and misunderstandings often experienced?]

Idea for Discussion: Some people seem to get along well without "close friends." Instead they have acquaintances, work companions, social companions, clients, neighbors, fellow community members, and so on. Perhaps they would be better off if they had close friends as well, but that doesn't seem to be crucial.

[*Discussion*: Do people miss out on something by not having close friends? What is a close friend anyway? Do people vary in the degree of closeness needed in a relationship?]

Principle for Discussion: Given the values which friendship (close or otherwise) appears to serve, **we should work at friendships.** We should not merely let them happen, but should be active in initiating and maintaining them.

[*Activity and Questions*: Make a list of ways to work at friendships: for example, writing letters when a friend goes away, phoning someone when we don't feel like it, keeping a date even though someone more interesting has come along, and so on. Do you agree that we should work at friendships, or does it seem unrealistic and unnatural? Do *you* in fact work at friendships? If not, should you?]

Principle for Discussion: We should only work at a friendship if it is a good friendship and worthwhile, all things considered. This is not necessarily a self-centred principle, since a major reason for maintaining a friendship is its value to the other person.

[*Activity and Questions*: Think of a time when you or someone else let a friendship end because it was not sufficiently worthwhile. Do you think it was the right thing to do? Are there times when we should work at a friendship even though it's not worthwhile? Should we ever work to maintain a friendship which does very little (or nothing) for us but is very important for the other person?]

Principle for Discussion: While friendships are valuable, we should not make an absolute out of friendship. It is just one value, to be weighed against others. For example, sometimes we should not try to keep up a friendship when circumstances change. Often we feel guilty about this but do nothing about it. Should we do something; or just stop feeling guilty? Here are some examples. What should be done in each case (depending on the precise circumstances)?

- You have been close friends with someone since early childhood. They go to live in a city far away, and you can only keep in touch with them by letter or an occasional brief telephone call.

- You have been close friends with someone who was a neighbor but moves to another suburb or town, ten miles away.

- A good friend of yours, a colleague at work, gets a different kind of job in another factory.

- Two people in their twenties have been friends for many years. One gets married and has children and develops many new interests, activities, and friends.

[*Discussion*: Should we keep up old friendships because they are old? What are some of the advantages of old friendships? Have you sometimes made a new friendship which seems as good as or even better than an old one? Do you feel guilty about not keeping up old friendships? Why?]

Idea for Discussion: Friendships usually (always?) have limitations or imperfections. It is important to develop values which enable us to accept at least some of these shortcomings; otherwise we may lose or spoil friendships which are not perfect but have much to offer. Here are some "realities" of friendship.

- Friends sometimes take advantage of (or "exploit") each other, consciously or unconsciously.

- A single friend, even one to whom we are utterly committed, is often not enough; even that friendship may be better — and deeper — if we have other friends as well.

- Even close friends are not always completely loyal to each other: a friend will sometimes criticize us behind our back or help someone else before us.

- Not all friends continue to need or even like each other: not all friendships are forever.

- Complete trust in a friend is not always justified.

- Complete frankness with a friend is not always wise.

[*Discussion*: Do you agree that these are realities of friendship? Should we accept them, or try to avoid friendships with characteristics of these kinds? What are the value implications of deciding to live with these realities?]

Idea for Discussion: One of the key values of friendship is dependence. We admit that it's all right to be in a dependent and trusting relationship with other human beings. We admit our need for companionship, affection, and help.

[*Discussion and Activity*: Think of people in literature or real life who have resisted accepting their need for friendship. How, in your opinion, should they have modified their lives? Think of ways in which you yourself have unduly resisted being dependent on others. What might you do about it?]

Idea for Discussion: Dependence, however, has its dangers and limitations. For example, if we are too dependent on friends, they may take advantage of us, consciously or unconsciously; they may take us for granted and stop appreciating us; we may not be able to deal with losing them; we may not feel very good about ourselves; we may become too serious and uninteresting.

[*Discussion and Activity*: Can you think of cases where someone has been too dependent on a friend? If so, what problems has it created? Do you feel that you yourself are too dependent on one or more friends? If so, develop plans to do something about it.]

Idea for Discussion: Friendships are often spoiled because too much emphasis is placed on the value of "justice" or "equal contribution." Of course, *true* justice is crucial, and injustice is currently one of the main inhibitors of friendship, especially between people of different races, classes, genders, and so on. But sometimes the concept of justice is distorted, with a resulting negative impact on friendship. Here are some examples of "unequal contribution":

- Two friends enjoy each other's company a lot but one is much better organized than the other and arranges to get them into parties, shows, and so on.

- One of two friends has much more money than the other and nearly always pays for them both.

- One friend is very good at making conversation and keeps the other entertained all the time when they are together.
- One friend forms relationships easily and could have lots of friends, while the other is very dependent on this particular friendship and would be unhappy without it.

[*Discussion and Activity*: Are these good friendships? Should they continue? Make a list of the various kinds of things people can contribute to a friendship. Think of cases — fictional or otherwise — where two people contribute different things to their friendship.]

VALUES AND STRESS

Definition: The word "stress," in everyday speech, is value laden. It usually refers to a case where things have gone *too far*, beyond desirable levels of worry, pressure, tension, or fear. "Stress" implies that pressure has reached a harmful, painful, or otherwise undesirable level.

[*Discussion:* What does the word "stress" mean to you?]

Key Idea: Stress is bad because of its consequences. These include pain, both direct and indirect; the inability to do what we want and need to do; difficulties in relationships; and physical and mental illness. Such consequences interfere with the attainment of well-being or the good life.

[*Activity*: Think of specific examples of consequences of stress you have experienced or seen in others.]

Idea for Discussion: A major cause of stress is lack of a sound value system. Inadequate values can lead to stress; and sound values can help alleviate stress. It's a mistake, then, to rely only on psychological and pharmacological measures in dealing with stress. Often we should apply "value therapy"! Here are some ways in which a poorly developed value system causes stress:

i. *We pursue goals that are not sufficiently worthwhile,* and then become upset at the pointlessness of what we are doing. For example:

   (a) We choose a job that is very time-consuming and yet is not interesting and doesn't pay well.

   (b) We do a university degree even though it's not leading anywhere and we would be much happier doing something else.

   (c) We get into personal relationships that involve a lot of work and conflict without much reward.

ii. *We pursue goals we can't achieve,* and then become tense in situations we can't handle and worried at the prospect of failure. For example:

   (a) A person runs for parliament but is not good at making convincing speeches or chatting with voters.

   (b) A writer has decided to turn out twenty books in her/his lifetime and then sees that time is running out.

(c) A person with a not particularly good voice tries to make a career as a singer.

iii. *We pursue conflicting goals,* and experience the tension of being pulled in different directions. For example:

(a) A person decides to have a large family and to take on a career that leaves little time or opportunity for family life.

(b) A union organizer tries to get on well with fellow workers and with the boss at the same time.

(c) A person wants to be a great athlete and a regular party-goer at the same time.

iv. *We pursue too many goals,* perhaps all of them very worthwhile, and find ourselves unable to cope with them. For example:

(a) A musician tries to be a great performer, conductor, composer, and teacher and is unable to fill all of these roles at once.

(b) A student takes on many different subjects and tries to do well at all of them in the same year.

(c) A person tries to have a very full social life, get a lot of reading done, keep fit, and start a new business all at once.

[*Activity and Discussion*: Find other examples of ways in which lack of a sound value system can result in stress. Do you agree that we sometimes rely too much on psychological and pharmacological measures in dealing with stress?]

Principle for Discussion: People can reduce stress by PRIORITIZING their values. In this way they can know that what they are doing is important, and they can also reduce overload by cutting out unimportant things. For example:

i. In our job, we can eliminate some activities completely, and change the proportion of time we spend on other activities. Also, we can add new, important activities.

ii. In personal budgeting, we can reduce spending in some areas, increase it in others, and, through an overall reduction, decrease the pressure to earn money.

iii. We can have priorities in how much time we spend with different people.

iv. We can have priorities in which parties and other social and group gatherings we go to.

v. We can have priorities in our hobbies. Which ones take up the most time? Which ones do we get the most out of?

vi. We can have priorities in reading and watching TV. How much time should we spend reading the newspaper? How much time should we spend watching TV? What kinds of programs should we watch the most?

vii. We can have priorities in what we want to achieve in life.

[*Discussion.* Discuss whether, in each of the above examples, this prioritizing is possible and whether it would reduce stress. Think of and discuss other examples where you could reduce stress by having priorities and being more careful about what you take on.]

Ideas for Discussion: We can reduce stress by AVOIDING activities and situations we find stressful. This is not necessarily a sign of weakness; indeed, *avoidance can be an act of moral courage, and result in great benefits for ourselves and others.* Whether it's right or wrong depends on the *values* at stake in each case. Here are some examples:

i. A lawyer who finds courtroom appearances too stressful could keep mainly to other kinds of legal work.

ii. A person who finds certain kinds of parties too stressful could come late and leave early, or simply not go at all.

iii. A pilot who finds solo flying too stressful could concentrate mainly on co-pilot work.

iv. A farmer who tends to worry a lot about the weather could keep to kinds of farming that are largely unaffected by weather conditions.

v. A football player who has found the pressure of being captain of the team too much could become just an ordinary member of the team.

vi. A business person who finds press interviews too stressful could hire a press relations person or communicate mainly by means of press releases.

vii. A parent who finds birthday parties in the home too stressful could arrange an outing or some other kind of celebration.

viii. A baby-sitter who finds looking after young babies too stressful could just look after children.

ix. People who find changing their place of residence too stressful could turn down offers of promotion in order to stay in the same area.

[*Discussion and Activity*: Discuss the above examples. Do you think avoidance of the stressful activity could be legitimate in each case? Think of stressful activities or situations you have avoided in the past or should avoid in the future. Discuss and assess your reasons.]

VALUES AND WORK

Definition: The word "work" is used broadly to refer to many kinds of sustained, purposeful activity which is not performed simply for pleasure. Here, however, we are mainly concerned with work in the sense of one's job or jobs.

[*Discussion*: What do the words "work," "job," and "leisure" mean to you?]

Key Idea: There are many values we can find in a job.

- Interest and enjoyment

- Sense of achievement and fulfilment
- Sense of making a contribution to society, helping other people
- Sense of meaning and purpose in life
- Status, recognition
- Money and other material benefits
- Self-development: extension of interests, knowledge, skills, awareness
- Togetherness, colleagueship, friendship (perhaps)
- Sense of belonging, security, continuity
- Physical exercise (perhaps)

[*Discussion and Activity*: What would you add to this list or delete from it? Why? Try to think of at least one job which has *all* these values. Think of jobs which do *not* have all these values.]

Key Idea: Whether or not a job has these values depends partly on the person in the job.

[*Activities:*

(a) Think of ways in which people put these values into their jobs. Discuss how you would put some of these values into your job or into a job you are planning to take up.

(b) Think of cases where people try hard to put some of these values into their job but aren't able to do so.

(c) Think of cases where people can't stick at *any* job because they can't find one that has enough value in it for them.]

Key Idea: Many jobs could be changed so that they would serve more values of the kind discussed above. For example:

i. In factories, people could be allowed to do a wider range of tasks so their work would be more interesting and fulfilling.

ii. More emphasis could be placed on joint decision-making so workers would feel more involved and fulfilled and have a greater sense of colleagueship.

iii. More emphasis could be placed on the societal significance of what workers do, so they could see how their work helps other people.

iv. Companies and institutions could encourage their employees to broaden their interests and abilities through courses, workshops, and staff training generally.

v. Workers could be encouraged and given facilities to take some form of exercise on the work premises, during breaks.

vi. Companies and institutions could increase their benefits to employees so they would have a greater sense of security and belonging.

vii. Companies and institutions could provide more facilities and encouragement for socializing among employees and between employees and employers.

[*Discussion*:

(a) Some of these things are already done in different parts of the world. Are there particular examples you have heard of? Do you think these changes are a good idea?

(b) What other ways are there of making jobs serve more values for people?

(c) Do you think society can afford changes of this kind, or would it be better to "let work remain work" and get our enjoyment and fulfilment elsewhere? Would some of these changes involve no cost at all? Of the rest, which would be more costly and which less?]

Principle for Discussion: Work is not an absolute value, an end in itself. Rather it is a *means* to other values. The so-called "protestant work ethic" sees work as an absolute value, an end in itself: work is to be done without asking "why." But treating work as an end in itself can lead to many problems, such as the following:

i. On the job, bosses often adopt a harsh "hire and fire" attitude toward employees, making "getting the job done" the only thing that matters.

ii. Employees often just go on working without asking whether there might be some more enjoyable and enriching way to earn a living.

iii. People see work itself as so important that they don't think of ways to bring other values into the workplace.

iv. People who are "unemployed," do volunteer work, do unpaid work, or who don't need to "earn a living" are made to feel guilty or inferior.

v. People who have a job outside the home for which they are paid often feel they can make heavy demands on their spouse at home who doesn't "earn a living."

vi. Society in general often puts considerations of "work" and "productivity" before environmental values, aesthetic values, family values, and many other human values.

[*Discussion*:

(a) Do you agree that work is not an end in itself? Discuss these and other examples of how the idea that work is an end in itself creates problems. Have you seen examples of this sort of thing?

(b) People often confuse "work" with "earning money." Unpaid work is not seen as work. Do you have to be paid in order to be working? Discuss examples of unpaid activity that looks like "work" and paid activity that doesn't look like "work."

(c) If we give up the "protestant work ethic," might the disadvantages outweigh the benefits? Can society survive without such an ethic?]

Principle for Discussion: Home-making is a job which presents some difficulties but in which we can find a number of values.

Some Difficulties

i. In modern Western society, home-making is often a fairly lonely occupation.

ii. Home-making often involves a fairly high degree of drudgery: many boring tasks, unpleasant tasks, tasks which have to be done over and over again.

iii. At present, in many circles, home-making doesn't have as much status as a job outside the home.

Some values

i. In some ways, home-making can be a fairly flexible job.

ii. Home-makers can be their own boss.

iii. Some aspects of home-making such as decorating, cooking, carpentry, gardening, entertaining, and so on, can be very interesting and fulfilling, depending on our temperament, abilities, and resources.

iv. Child rearing, where it is part of home-making, can be an interesting and fulfilling activity, and can make a contribution to society.

[*Discussion*: How can the difficulties of home-making be reduced and the values increased? Should our society try to restore the status that running a household used to have? Would you like to be a home-maker for much or all of your adult life? Should home-makers be paid a salary? Should home-making be seen as a job in the popular sense?]

Idea for Discussion: In two-adult families, the respective spouses should share the home-making equally, although the work assigned to each should depend on their interests and abilities.

Some problems

i. It's sometimes difficult to find a suitable job outside the home that leaves us with enough time and energy to be even a half-time home-maker.

ii. Some people feel that the modern idea that we should be able to have an outside job is undermining even more the status of home-making. Having a spouse share this role only makes matters worse.

[*Discussion*: Do you think that sharing the home-making role makes things better or worse? Can this be a good arrangement for some people? Can the difficulties of this arrangement be overcome?]

VALUES AND HEALTH

Ideas for Discussion:

(a) **Health is a basic value, which we pursue partly AS AN END IN ITSELF.** Especially in infancy, we have some instinctive tendencies to seek foods and activities which are good for our health. And throughout life we show instinctive pain and injury avoidance behavior.

(b) **Health is also a MEANS to many other important values.** Health serves happiness in that it reduces pain and is the basis of many pleasant feelings. Health obviously is important in achieving survival. And good health gives us greater capacity to pursue a range of other values.

[*Activities*:

(a) Find examples of cases where we pursue health partly as an end in itself, without thinking much about other values.

(b) Find examples of cases where health is a means to other values].

Principle for Discussion: A sound system of values is a necessary basis for health. Here are some ways in which sound values promote health:

i. Enjoyment, satisfaction, and happiness arising out of the successful pursuit of basic values help keep us healthy.

ii. A sense of meaning and worthwhileness in life, related to well worked out values, makes us more resistant to illness.

iii. The "stroking" and sense of being appreciated and loved associated with good human relationships promotes good health.

iv. Stress reduction through well worked out values helps us avoid stress-related illnesses such as stomach ulcers, heart disease, back pain, headaches, listlessness, and the pain of stress itself.

v. A well-planned, well-directed way of life can give us the time, energy, and resources we need for health maintenance.

[*Activities*:

(a) Think of cases you have heard or read about where having sound values has helped people's health, or where not having sound values has resulted in illness.

(b) Think of ways in which changes in your values and way of life could improve your health or help prevent you from becoming ill.]

Principle for Discussion: While health is to SOME extent an end in itself, it is not an absolute value: it must be weighed against other values. Some people take health *too* seriously. Here are some examples of choices that have to be made at times between health and other values.

i. The mental pain of a strict diet may not be worth it, for a particular patient.

ii. The financial cost to a patient of a particular treatment may not be worth it.

iii. The timing of treatment may make the cure worse than the illness.

iv. The effort involved in doing exercises to cure an illness may not be worth it.

v. For some people, the time involved in maintaining a high level of general fitness may not be justified in light of their overall set of values.

vi. The side effects of a treatment may rule it out for some people depending on their other values.

vii. Some people, depending on their other values, may prefer a risky operation which promises complete recovery to a less risky and less complete cure.

viii. The effects of certain illnesses — and cures — on a person's physical appearance must be taken into account.

ix. The degree of pain of an illness must be weighed in deciding whether to live with the illness or try to cure it.

x. There are many activities that aren't particularly good for our health — mountain climbing, working in a disease-ridden country, being a politician, heavy partying — which may nevertheless be appropriate, at least for a time, given our other values. Some people *do* want to "burn their candle at both ends," and for them, at a given time, it may be right to do so.

[*Discussion*: Discuss the above examples — and others you can think of — and the general principle that health is not an absolute and must be weighed against other values. Do you agree with the principle?]

Key Concept: Optimal Level of Health. Try to work out for yourself what your "optimal" level of health is, that is, the *appropriate* level of health for you, given all your other values. Then, for each aspect of your optimal health level, work out how you will achieve (or maintain) it.

Principle for Discussion: The authority of a doctor, nurse, or other health professional is not an absolute value: other people must have a say, especially the patient. Here are some arguments for this principle:

i. There are so many personal value issues involved in medical decisions that the patient must have a major say in what is done (or not done).

ii. Patients should be involved more than at present in diagnosis, since they know a great deal about their own bodies and could, with encouragement and training, become even more adept at sensing what is going on inside them.

iii. Patients can often see better than health professionals the context and possible causes of illness in their total way of life.

iv. In a joint, interactive relationship, health professionals learn much more and so are better equipped to help patients.

[*Discussion*: Do you agree with these arguments, and with the general principle? Think of cases where the wishes of the patient (and perhaps family and friends) are especially important. Do you think patients should feel free to seek second and third medical opinions rather than accept the judgment of a single doctor?]

Key Idea: Preventive health care requires value decisions at both an individual and a societal level. A well-developed value system is needed to enable us to make sound decisions in this area.

[*Discussion*: How much do you believe in preventive health care? Here are some examples of preventive health care. For each example, weigh the values involved and say what you would be willing to do.

i. *Regular exercise*. What kinds of exercise? How often? How many hours a week?

ii. *Sleep, relaxation, stress reduction*. What kinds? How often? How long?

iii. *Nutrition, dieting*. Which foods and drinks would you avoid? Which would you plan to have? How much time, effort, self-regulation would you be willing to put into it?

iv. *Dental check-ups, cleaning*. How often? How much?

v. *Life planning*. So you will have the time, energy, resources for health maintenance, relaxation, and so on. What kind? How much?

vi. *Personal environmental control*. To avoid noise pollution, atmospheric pollution, food pollution, overcrowding, and so on. What kinds? How much?

vii. *Public environmental control*. What kinds? At what expense? How much time and effort would you personally be prepared to devote to it?]

Key Idea: Many value issues concerning life and death arise in modern health care. Once again, this requires us to have a well-developed value system.

[*Discussion*: What should be done in these cases?

i. A doctor is convinced that a patient has only three or four months left to live, and is wondering what to tell the patient and close relatives.

ii. A terminally ill cancer patient is in great pain and has requested an increased dosage of morphine. The drug would reduce the pain but would also reduce the life expectancy of the patient.

iii. A terminally ill patient can have the pain greatly reduced by an operation that would also reduce brain function and awareness generally.

iv. A patient is in a coma and is being kept alive by machines. There is no hope of recovery and the life support procedures are very expensive. The patient's family is poor and is not covered by any medical scheme. They will have to work for many years to pay the medical bills.

v. A very elderly patient is hospitalized with a number of serious illnesses and life expectancy is short. Heart failure occurs and various procedures are tried to get the heart beating again. The only possibilities remaining are brutal forms of heart stimulation.

vi. A particular country can only afford a limited number of artificial kidney machines, and decisions must be made about who will have access to these machines. Some people can pay much of the cost of their treatment, others very little. Some patients will die if a machine is not available for them. The patients vary greatly in age.

vii. A woman in advanced pregnancy learns that, according to quite reliable tests, her child will be severely handicapped. She requests that the fetus be aborted.

viii. A pregnant woman develops an illness connected with her pregnancy that could endanger her life. She requests an abortion.]

VALUES AND THE AESTHETIC SIDE OF LIFE

Idea for Discussion: Aesthetic pleasure and satisfaction is a value area which requires closer attention. In Western societies there are two problems with it at present. (1) We have greatly neglected this value area in private and public life. (2) We have failed to see aesthetics in the context of our total value system, having pursued it in isolation from other values.

[*Discussion and Activity*: Do you agree that aesthetics needs greater emphasis, in both private and public life? If so, think of examples of ugliness or simply absence of aesthetic pleasure in modern life. Think of ways in which this could be changed. Make plans to emphasize the aesthetic side of life more.]

Key Question: What things do you get aesthetic pleasure or satisfaction from? Here is a possible list:

books
films
TV
plays
pictures

ceremonies
architecture
sculpture
furniture
scenery

music	trees and plants
parties	animals
people	clothes
etc.	

[*Activity and Discussion*: Decide what you wish to add to or delete from the above list. For each item on your final list (a) indicate how important it is to you as a source of aesthetic enjoyment (for example, not very; fairly; very), and (b) note specific examples of what gives you aesthetic enjoyment (for example, guitar music; religious ceremonies; mountain scenery). Discuss your opinions and experiences with others.]

Idea for Discussion: Aesthetic pleasures and satisfactions are of great practical value in our lives. They give us contentment and a sense of meaning in life even when other things are not going well. Also, we can often have them even when we are short of money.

[*Activities*:

(1) Look again at your list of aesthetic objects and specific examples. Find there examples of aesthetic things you do (a) when you want to feel better about life, and (b) when you are short of money. Do you agree that aesthetic pleasures and satisfactions are of great practical value in our lives?

(2) Think of (a) actual, (b) fictitious, or (c) possible examples of people who, at various times and in various circumstances, have gained pleasure, contentment, or a sense of meaning in life through aesthetic experience. Here are some possible examples.

i. People in war camps who had little else to do but read or draw.

ii. People during the 1930s Depression who could only afford inexpensive pastimes.

iii. Young people who cannot afford a car with a stereo and so walk around with head sets listening to music.

iv. People in dentists' waiting rooms who read magazine articles instead of thinking about the treatment they are about to receive.

Add further examples of your own.]

Principle for Discussion: We should be preparing now for kinds of aesthetic experience that will be valuable for us later in life.

[*Discussion and Activity*: Do you agree with this principle? Can you think of younger or older adults who have problems because they don't seem to have enough aesthetic interests and capacities? If you agree with the principle, draw up plans for the next six months or the next three years for preparing for your aesthetic needs in later life.]

Principle for Discussion: It is important, where possible, to find or create objects and activities in life which COMBINE aesthetic values with other values. Here are some possible examples:

i. Books which are both intellectually stimulating and a pleasure to read.

ii. Magazine and newspaper articles which are both informative and well written.

iii. A home which is both convenient and as attractive as we can make it.

iv. Clothes which as far as possible combine economy, functionality, and style.

v. A job which pays well, is fulfilling and useful, and is aesthetically pleasing and enriching in as many ways as possible.

[*Discussion*: Do you agree with the general principle? If so, can you think of other examples?]

Principle for Discussion: Tradition and aesthetics are closely linked: we need advice from the past on how to create and enjoy beauty. For example:

i. In order to cook well, we use recipes passed down from generation to generation.

ii. Good painting usually draws on centuries of tradition, whether consciously or not.

iii. In order to enjoy good music — even "popular" music — we have to have experience of a tradition of musical expression.

iv. In order to write well, we need to study and experience forms of written and oral expression that have historical links.

v. In order to make a beautiful film, we must be familiar with traditions of film making and other forms of expression.

[*Discussion*: Discuss these and other examples. Do you agree with the general principle?]

Key Question: How can we avoid just sticking to the past in aesthetic matters?

[*Activities:*

(a) Think of cases where sticking too much to the past has undermined creativity, aesthetic pleasure, and other values.

(b) Think of ways in which we can link up with the past in creating and enjoying beauty and at the same time create new trends and adapt traditions to our present needs.

(c) Think of examples of people or things which show that this is possible.

(d) Specifically, identify films and books which are aesthetically pleasing and have a mixture of the traditional and the new.]

Idea for Discussion: We don't have to excel in something to get aesthetic enjoyment from it. For example:

i. We don't have to be great violinists to enjoy playing the violin.

ii. We don't have to be great artists to enjoy drawing.

iii. We don't have to be great dancers to learn dancing and enjoy it.

[*Discussion and Activities:*

(a) Do you agree with the idea for discussion? If so, think of other things we can enjoy aesthetically without excelling in.

(b) Think of examples of people in film or literature — or whom you know — who are strong artistically but don't seem to enjoy their art very much; and people of mediocre artistic ability who seem to enjoy it a lot.

(c) Make concrete plans to take up some activity which you think you will enjoy aesthetically even though you probably won't excel in it.]

Idea for Discussion: The difficulty of what we do is often not as important as the beauty with which we do it. For example:

i. A simple piece of music played beautifully may bring much more pleasure to ourselves and our friends than a difficult piece played without tone or feeling.

ii. A ceremony need not be very complex or difficult to perform in order to be beautiful.

[*Discussion and Activity*:

(a) Discuss these examples and think of other cases where beauty can be achieved without a high level of "technical skill." Do you agree with the idea for discussion?

(b) Make concrete plans to increase the beauty of something you do without necessarily increasing its technical difficulty.]

VALUES AND FAMILY LIFE

Idea for Discussion: The family serves a wide range of values:

- affection
- protection and health care
- training in life skills
- social and intellectual training
- cultural, moral, and religious training
- human contact
- a home base
- a sense of belonging
- privacy
- material needs — food, clothing, shelter, transport, money, and so on.

[*Discussion Activity*:

(a) Do you agree that the family serves these values? How well does it do so? Discuss examples for some or all of the values.

(b) Work out a number of different kinds of families — just a mother with child(ren), just a father with child(ren), and so on — that you have seen or can imagine. For each kind, can the values listed above be served? Do you see any difficulties? What about adoption? Do you think it is important that children be brought up by their biological parent(s)?]

Idea for Discussion: People vary in the extent to which they need other people. Some, for example, seem to be able to live quite happily as hermits, alone in the mountains or woods. Many are living very well today as "singles," without spouse or children: they may need other people but their family needs appear to be limited.

[*Activity and Discussion*: Think of examples of people who need others more and people who need others less. Work out what are the differences here in temperament, circumstances, and so on. Is it alright to need other people a great deal? Is it alright not to need other people very much?]

Statement for Discussion: "From middle childhood onward, many people question the value of their family. However, in most cases, we should continue to maintain fairly close contact with our parental family. For one thing, we continue to need it in most of the ways discussed earlier. But apart from that, we have little choice. Our family is so much part of us that we can't escape it. We need to understand our parent(s) and sibling(s) in order to understand ourselves. We must *make* our family relationships work, to an extent, because in both the short and long run it's worth it."

[*Discussion*:

(a) What do you think of this statement? Discuss it in some detail.

(b) Can you think of cases where people *should* considerably reduce contact with their parental family? If so, in what ways should they reduce contact, and in what ways should they try to maintain contact?]

Principle for Discussion: We should not usually attempt to change our family but, rather, accept them and enjoy them (as far as possible) as they are. Trying to change people is in general a risky venture. In the family it often does much more harm than good. Here are some ways of accepting and enjoying our family:

i. Concentrate on those things we do enjoy doing with our family or discussing with them.

ii. Often, simply avoid situations and discussion we dislike.

iii. Where we can't resist objecting to something, do it as a personal expression rather than to teach or change.

iv. Work out ways of protecting ourselves from our family without hurting someone else in the family.

[*Discussion*: Discuss specific ways in which we might implement these techniques in the family. Think of kinds of things we should accept in other family members rather than try to change. Think of things that should be changed.]

Principle for Discussion: Expressions of negative emotion — anger, frustration, dislike, disapproval, and so on — are often necessary in the family, but they mustn't be taken too far. They are often necessary because:

i. We need to get our concern off our chest.

ii. The other person(s) may not know how we feel, and *some* change may be possible.

iii. If we share our thoughts and feelings, we may develop a deeper relationship.

However, we mustn't go too far because:

i. "What is said can never be unsaid."

ii. Our chief concern should be to accept rather than judge or change.

iii. An exaggerated statement or reaction, in the heat of the moment, can lead to misunderstanding and painful, unnecessary argument.

iv. Telling people negative things we think or feel about them sometimes does no good at all and often makes things worse.

[*Activity and Discussion*:

(a) Think of examples where expressing a negative emotion in the family is important. Do you agree with the idea for discussion?

(b) Think of a time when you felt angry toward one or more members of your family. What did you say/do? Was that the best response?]

Idea for Discussion: Family relationships present unusual difficulties, which require us to get some distance, while remaining close. Recognition of these problems, as early as possible, can help us overcome them. For example:

i. *Sibling rivalry*. Children of the same family often compete too much with each other. They need to see each other more as distinctive, ordinary people, each with their own mark to make in the world.

ii. *Parent–child rivalry*. Parents and children often feel that they must be "better" than each other. Again, they need to see each other as human beings in their own right, without making undue comparisons.

iii. *Emotional blackmail*. Family members sometimes do things for each other just out of a sense of guilt, when what is done is not really necessary or right. We should try not to use or give in to this kind of blackmail, but rather look at the situation more objectively.

iv. *People who don't like each other very much*. People may belong to the same family but not be "kindred spirits." Family members must gradually work out what kind of friendship relationships they are going to have with each other in the context of the family relationship.

v. *Shift in the parental role*. In the early years, a parent must be teacher, guide, and protector. In later years, the attempt to continue this role too much can be disastrous. A gradual, difficult shift must take place.

[*Discussion*: Discuss some or all of the above problems and try in each case to work out how to deal with it. Do you think that, despite such problems, family relationships are still worthwhile?]

Idea for Discussion: Reduction in extended family and close community life has created many problems. The nuclear family — just a single family unit with parent(s) and child(ren) — has many disadvantages. For example:

i. People feel lonely.

ii. Spouses are too dependent on each other, emotionally, economically, and so on.

iii. Children don't have as many people close to them to be friends with and learn from.

iv. Old people are more cut off from middle-aged people and children, in particular from their own children and grandchildren.

v. It's more difficult to get help with baby-sitting and day-care.

vi. It's more difficult to get help when things go wrong.

[*Discussion*: Do you agree that there are these problems associated with nuclear families? Can you think of other problems?]

Idea for Discussion: The nuclear family, however, has some advantages. For example:

i. Greater privacy.

ii. Greater freedom.

iii. Greater mobility.

[*Discussion*:

(a) Do you agree that there are these advantages? Can you think of others? Do you think the advantages of a nuclear family outweigh the disadvantages? Why?

(b) What are some of the factors that have led people toward nuclear families and away from extended families and close communities? Do you think it was right for people to be influenced by these factors? *In what direction should we go now?*]

Idea for Discussion: Extended families and close communities are difficult to maintain if businesses and other institutions require employees to be constantly on the move. We must look at the recruitment, promotion, and transfer policies in our society to see if they take family and community considerations into account sufficiently.

[*Discussion*: Do you think the human cost of the recruitment, promotion, and transfer policies in our society is too high? Do you think employees themselves think enough about the problems of moving from one region to another?]

Idea for Discussion: Extended families and close communities are difficult to maintain if builders, architects, and residential planners don't take their needs into account. For example:

i. Houses, even quite large ones, are often built in such a way that it is difficult to have a semi-private area for grandparents, teenagers, or other members of an extended family.

ii. High-rise apartment buildings and high-density townhouse developments often lack the facilities for community members to meet each other and do things together.

iii. Suburban housing areas, too, often lack the parks, small shopping centres, entertainment centres, and other public facilities needed by a close community.

[*Discussion and Activities*:

(a) Can you think of specific examples of these problems? Can you think of other ways in which architecture and residential planning have made it difficult to have extended families and close communities? What can be done about this problem (i) in attempting to use existing buildings and (ii) in attempting to control building projects more in the future?

(b) Work out an ideal pattern of family and community life for people such as yourself which decreases the disadvantages and increases the advantages of nuclear family, extended family, and close community membership.

(c) List some ways (if any) in which you plan to increase or decrease your extended family and close community participation in the next year, the next ten years, the next forty years.]

Part Four:

Learning and Teaching Values in Adulthood

Part Four begins with an exploration of ways in which adults learn values (in Chapter 12), and then proceeds to an examination of a number of historical and contemporary approaches to values education (in Chapter 13). It is shown how each of these approaches, while making a contribution, is too narrow. At the end of Chapter 13 a plea is made for a much more comprehensive approach to values education, incorporating the insights of the ones reviewed and also going beyond them. In Chapter 14 some new directions for adult values education are discussed, with special reference to the need for dialogue.

CHAPTER 12

How Adults Learn Values

Before going on in Chapters 13 and 14 to discuss values education, in this chapter we will look at how we *learn* values. This will help individuals in their personal learning. It will also help show the constraints under which the teaching of values takes place, and give some hints about successful educational method. The words "learn" and "learning" here are being used broadly to include acquiring emotions, attitudes, dispositions, and behavior patterns, as well as beliefs and concepts. The terms "teaching" and "education" are equally broad.

This survey of ways in which we learn values is obviously not exhaustive. What I will do is outline some elements which, in my view, are particularly important or have in the past been neglected. Further, it should be noted that while this discussion is of *adult* learning, I'm not suggesting that the principles presented are only relevant to adults. The same principles could, I believe, also be applied to children's values learning.

Incremental Learning

One of the most important principles of values learning is that of *accepting and building incrementally on a person's existing value system*. This is closely linked to the general educational principle of moving from the known to the unknown. As Shakespeare said in *King Lear*, "nothing will come of nothing." And as John Dewey emphasized repeatedly, learning is like growth in that what comes later must largely emerge from and incorporate what was before.

Speaking specifically of moral learning, Dewey explains that morality doesn't produce a discontinuity between pre-existing values and moral good, but rather an appropriate modification within an ongoing stream of valuing.

> There is a contrast between the natural goods — those which appeal to immediate desire — and the moral good, that which is approved after reflection. But the difference is not absolute and inherent. The moral good is some natural good which is sustained and developed through consideration of its relations . . . .[1]

David Smail, in his discussion of the limitations of therapy, says that the marks left on us by past experience are largely unalterable and must be seen as a starting point rather than something to be changed. He says:

> To try to alter people's experience after they have acquired it is a bit like trying to control the weight of battery chickens by surgery. . . . The fact is that people are organisms and their experience is acquired organically, and so deeply and inextricably

1. J. Dewey, *Theory of Moral Life* (New York: Holt, Rinehart and Winston, 1960; originally 1932), p. 56.

> bound up is it with the very structures of the body that erasure of the experience would entail destruction of the organism. We cannot, like magnetic tape, be wiped clean of our history, which is, on the contrary, acquired as are the growth rings of a tree.[2]

Clarifying the implications of this for future development, Smail goes on:

> I do not want to say that people are incapable of developing or modifying experience as they go through life, but that such development or modification must fit in with and grow out of what has gone before — it must be organic. People *grow* from one position to the next, they cannot be *switched*.[3]

A gnarled tree may be transplanted to more hospitable surroundings and in an important sense "flourish." But if it is to flourish, its earlier characteristics must largely be accepted and indeed utilized as the basis for future growth.

We noted in Chapters 2 and 3 that everyone already has a value system fairly well adapted to their distinctive personality and life circumstances. When we are *strongly* critical of other people's life-style it is usually because it has especially negative consequences for us, or because we don't understand it. While there is always room for improvement, this can't be achieved — in ourselves or others — if present values are totally rejected. We must build — incrementally — on what is.

Socrates, undoubtedly overstating the case, maintained long ago that people don't knowingly act contrary to the

2. D. Smail, *Taking Care: An Alternative to Therapy* (London: Dent, 1987), pp. 87-88.
3. *Ibid.*, p. 89. His italics.

good. They have reasons for what they do. While people may not always choose the best alternatives, they usually choose quite good ones, under the circumstances. The task of values learning is not to find a completely new approach to life, but to modify and fine-tune an approach which already has considerable merit. This is in line with "hermeneutic" thought, to be discussed in Chapter 14, which sees us reinterpreting and developing an existing tradition rather than imposing a totally new way of life from outside. As David Kolb says:

> Everyone enters every learning situation with more or less articulate ideas about the topic at hand. We are all psychologists, historians, and atomic physicists. It is just that some of our theories are more crude and incorrect than others.[4]

One implication of an incremental approach which largely accepts people's current values is that an educator must proceed by *dialogue* rather than preaching or imposition. For learners' insights into their present situation and way of life are crucial in developing future directions. This doesn't mean we simply sit around and chat about values; as I will claim in Chapter 14, it is often important for teachers (and learners) to state and argue passionately for a particular point of view. However, we must listen as much as we speak, keen to find out the other person's views and modify our position as necessary in light of this feedback.

Our acceptance of people's current values will also be reflected in a *sympathetic manner*, largely devoid of blame and scolding. There is more than one reason for this. Not only is it appropriate given that people are acting in good faith and usually rather sensibly. It's also important

4. D. Kolb, *Experiential Learning* (Englewood Cliffs, N.J.: Prentice-Hall, 1984), p. 28.

because people who are approached in a hostile, critical manner become defensive, and their ability to learn is reduced; indeed, they may be reinforced in their present outlook.

Madhu Suri Prakash has developed this point, noting that "in order to expedite authentic change of a positive nature, we (must) give up trying to directly convert others through argument, praise, or condemnation."[5] Prakash quotes Carl Rogers who states that "the curious paradox is . . . we cannot change, we cannot move away from what we are, until we thoroughly accept what we are. Then change seems to come about, almost unnoticed."[6] Of course, there is some place for evaluating and "judging" the lives of others if they are to learn from us (and we from them). As we saw in Chapter 2, people can make mistakes in value matters. Prakash acknowledges this, explaining her position as follows:

> Part of the difficulty lies in the ambiguity of words such as "evaluate," "judge," and "suggest." One can do these things in a negative, "judgmental," overbearing manner or in a positive, constructive, compassionate manner. One can evaluate in a way that implies moral blame or in a spirit of offering help in solving a difficult problem. Evaluation of the first kind is ruled out on both theoretical and practical grounds. . . . But evaluation of the second kind — constructive and compassionate — would appear to

5. M. Prakash, "'Desires' Clarified, Much of 'Value': A Plea for Values Clarification," *Journal of Moral Education*, Vol. 17, No. 2 (May 1988), p. 22.
6. C. Rogers, *On Becoming a Person* (Boston: Houghton Mifflin Co., 1961), p. 17.

be necessary, at least to a degree, in a helping relationship.[7]

Concrete, Problem-Centred Learning

A common view in the West has been that we learn values by acquiring a handful of general principles — for example, the Golden Rule and the Ten Commandments — which we then apply to specific cases. Indeed, sometimes people question whether values education is necessary at all since there is nothing, apart from these few principles, that we need to learn. In fact, however, each problem we face requires, in addition to principles, a great deal of specific knowledge and the application of many specific values. Much values learning, then, must deal with concrete problem areas.

Research on adult learning shows that adults usually *prefer* a problem-oriented approach.[8] Traditional discipline-oriented courses of study are seldom chosen unless they are required to obtain a diploma or degree. This may be because people in our society are not sufficiently aware of the practical value of theory. But theory, as it is developed and presented in our society, is indeed rarely of much practical help, at least in areas such as values. It would seem that, rather than asking people to accept "on faith" that value theory is important, we should *combine* the study of principles and concrete problems so that the relevance of the one to the other is obvious.

There is a two-way relationship between general principles and specific cases. Principles help bring to a situation insights from previous experience and from

7. M. Prakash and C. Beck, "Teaching Without Moralizing: The Teacher as Compassionate Witness," unpublished manuscript, 1986, pp. 34-35.
8. K. P. Cross, *Adults as Learners* (San Francisco: Jossey-Bass, 1981), pp. 193-94 and 207-208.

theory; but equally, grappling with concrete problems often leads us to modify our principles significantly. Far from being merely applied, value principles must continue to be refined throughout life. We can never have a full, perfect grasp of a value principle since further experience may show that its meaning must be changed in certain respects. The interaction between principles/theory and experience is described by Kolb as follows:

> Ideas are not fixed and immutable elements of thought but are formed and re-formed through experience.[9]
>
> Knowledge is continuously derived from and tested out in the experiences of the learner. (p. 27)
>
> [T]he process of experiential learning can be described as a four-stage cycle involving four adaptive learning modes — concrete experience, reflective observation, abstract conceptualization, and active experimentation. (p. 40)

Value principles must be modified not only in the light of new specific insights into life but also as a result of changes in our concrete life circumstances. The principle of "providing for the future," for example, will mean different things for a twenty-year-old and a seventy-year-old (although there will be commonalities). Similarly, the principle of "not taking on too much" will have a different meaning for someone in mid-adolescence and someone in late adulthood (although again with common elements). A value principle, once again, is not something with a fixed meaning into which we progressively gain more insight. Its very nature may vary at a fundamental level depending on the needs of those who use it; and even for the same person its meaning may have to be

9. *Experiential Learning*, p. 26.

modified many times throughout life. This doesn't mean that knowledge is purely relative or subjective, but rather that what is known keeps changing, requiring modification in our ideas about reality.

This problem-centred approach is rather different from that advanced by Lawrence Kohlberg. Kohlberg certainly realizes the need for tackling specific problems, claiming that it can help us see the inadequacy of our present moral structure and stimulate us to adopt a new one. However, Kohlberg presupposes a total moral structure which, when it changes, is modified across the whole range of a person's moral thinking. My view is that this type of "generalization" to all other problem areas simply doesn't happen. Values learning is much more problem-specific than that. For example, we may learn how to deal fairly with our students, while failing to do so with our spouse and children; or we may largely overcome prejudice toward one ethnic group while continuing to have it toward another.

The importance of considering concrete cases has been well argued by Nel Noddings. She uses many examples to establish the point that "rules cannot guide us infallibly."[10] Accordingly, an ethical person is "wary of rules and principles. She formulates and holds them loosely, tentatively, as economies of a sort, but she insists upon holding closely to the concrete. She wants to maintain and to exercise her receptivity" (p. 55).

The key ethical value of caring, then, is acquired largely through concrete experience. It "arises as a product of actual caring and being cared for and my reflection on the goodness of these concrete caring situations" (p. 84). Ethical teaching, accordingly, doesn't take place through the mere presentation of principles. As

10. N. Noddings, *Caring: A Feminine Approach to Ethics and Moral Education* (Berkeley: University of California Press, 1984), p. 55.

Noddings says: "The lessons in 'right' and 'wrong' are hard lessons — not swiftly accomplished by setting up as an objective the learning of some principle. We do not say: It is wrong to steal. Rather, we consider why it was wrong or may be wrong in this case to steal. . . . The one-caring . . . wants her child to consider the act itself in full context" (p. 93). It is possible that Noddings goes *too* far in playing down the significance of principles,[11] but her arguments for giving attention to concrete cases are certainly valid.

To a large extent, then, values learning must be in the context of specific problems. While general discussion of values is important, it must involve extensive consideration of examples. Accordingly, it will often be appropriate to establish learning programs dealing primarily with particular problem areas: for example, drugs, relationships, coping with stress, marriage, parenting, mid-life career change, caring for older parents, preparing for retirement, and so on. Such programs should include consideration of value theory and principles; but we should never stray too far from concrete issues.

Amateur Learning

People learn a great deal about values through their own everyday experiences and through reflecting on these and discussing them with family members, friends, and acquaintances. In this way, they are able to modify and elaborate the ideas passed on to them by society and arrive at a value system tailored to their particular needs and circumstances. They are also able to offer an original critique of values prevalent in society.

11. For a constructive critique of Noddings along these lines, see Isa Aron, "Caring and Principles: Opponents or Partners?", *Philosophy of Education 1988*, PES Proceedings, 1988, pp. 126-35.

What I am referring to here might appropriately be called "amateur learning." However, we mustn't equate amateur learning with "self-directed learning" in a narrow, individualistic sense. Amateur learning in fact often relies heavily on input from others, and may be experienced by a group as well as an individual. The main point about it is that it doesn't involve undue deference to professionals and experts, as if they were the main source of insight.[12]

We often underestimate the capacity of ordinary people to work successfully (as individuals or in groups) on their value problems. We should understand that, on the one hand, they have extensive *knowledge* of their own life situation and the needs, attitudes, and behavior patterns of the people around them. Accordingly, they are in a strong position to make wise judgments about how they should live. And on the other hand, they have great *motivation* to develop a sound value system, since they and their inner group are the ones who will be most directly affected by it. To adapt a popular saying: the one who wears the shoe knows where it pinches, and cares that it pinches.

In values learning, discussion with ordinary people around us is crucial. There is a tendency to go further afield for advice, partly because we are too proud to accept counsel from those near to us, and partly because we assume there must be gurus or experts who have *the* answer. Also, the suggestions of relatives and friends often seem obvious and limited. But we should realize that those near to us are in an especially good position to help us because they know us and our situation so well. Further, as we noted in Chapter 2, there is no such thing

12. Allen Tough documents the very large extent to which adult learners utilize non-professional help, especially of family and friends. See his *Intentional Changes* (Chicago: Follett, 1982), pp. 65-69.

as *the* answer to a value question, even from an expert; so if we can arrive at a somewhat better (though limited) solution through reflection and informal discussion close to home we may have done the best we can.

One problem with experts is that they usually can't devote enough time to us. As Smail says, speaking of therapeutic experts, "unlike (in ideal circumstances) family or friends, therapists play an only temporary role in the lives of almost all their patients, and their commitment to help is strictly limited in terms of their actual involvement in patients' lives (were this not so, the job would become demanding beyond endurance)."[13] Added to experts' lack of familiarity with our situation, then, is the further limitation of lack of time (not to mention other resources).

The use of self-help books may be seen as an extension of amateur learning. These are semi-professional products which contain hints, anecdotes, and examples from everyday experience and encourage people to try to solve their problems largely by themselves. Such books are sometimes disparaged by academics and professionals, but in fact they are legitimate in that they "help people to help themselves" (in a way that many experts, unfortunately, do not). There is a danger, it is true, that people will look to a particular self-help book (or a series of them, one after another) to provide *the* answer; but that is to miss the point of "self-help." Rather than steering people away from such books, we should help them learn to use them in moderation, as further grist for the mill of amateur learning.

13. *Taking Care*, pp. 85-86.

Social Learning

Apart from learning that is deliberately brought about by educators and by learners themselves as amateurs, values learning takes place through direct influence — for good and ill — by the society around us. Through society we have passed on to us sound value principles and ways of life established and tested over thousands of years of human experience. From society, also, we unwittingly absorb stereotypes, prejudices, mistaken assumptions, harmful attitudes, and damaging patterns of behavior. Humans are social beings who will always be directly influenced by each other. As Smail puts it: "There could be no more superfluous statement of the obvious than that . . . people are profoundly affected by other people."[14]

Liberal political, moral, and educational theory has exaggerated the extent to which we can reflect on and freely choose our value beliefs. Socialist theory, also, as Herbert Marcuse has shown, has been too optimistic about the wisdom of the masses. Adults of all stations in society are susceptible to the mind-numbing influences of received tradition, deliberate propaganda, and popular belief.[15] This doesn't negate the important role of individuals in attaining value insight; but it means that the efforts of individuals must be *complemented* by processes at a communal and societal level.

A difficulty here is that no matter how democratically we behave in attempting to change the values of individuals and society, we may eventually be accused of indoctrination. For we are participating in a system which, at certain points, doesn't operate through the free,

14. *Ibid.*, p. 84.
15. See, for example, H. Marcuse, *One-Dimensional Man* (Boston: Beacon Press, 1964); and *An Essay on Liberation* (Boston: Beacon Press, 1969).

informed choice of those whose values are being influenced. This fact, however, is one which I believe we must accept. While we should try to ensure that people are as aware as possible of the choices they make, we must work for values we believe in, realizing that if we don't intervene, others will nevertheless continue to promote their values through direct influence. Failure to act would suggest a lack of seriousness about values which we claim to be important. For example, it would be morally inappropriate, in my view, not to play a part in overcoming racist stereotypes in society simply because we realize that, in doing so, some of our influence will be direct. We should keep such influence to a minimum, but some will be inevitable.

Adults learn values not only through what is said in society but also through the way things are done: through the political, economic, legal, domestic, communal, and other structures of society. This happens in two main ways. On the one hand, we are influenced by the value *assumptions* implied by social structures. For example, if women are not paid for home-making activities, we assume these are less important; and if certain ethnic groups are consistently favored in appointments to public office, we assume they have superior abilities. On the other hand, social structures *force* us to adopt certain values, because our well-being depends in part on fitting in with the rest of society. For example, people who know that for health or other reasons they should work less and relax more nevertheless have great difficulty slowing down in a busy society. So long as they are expected to fulfil all those obligations, reach all those targets, have all those possessions, and *appear* to be busy, there is a limit to what individuals can realistically do unless they have an enormous capacity to be "outsiders," which creates problems of its own.

One option many individuals choose in trying to overcome undesirable societal influences is to join a sub-group such as a religious community, a housing co-operative, or a ghetto community. However, it is often difficult to find a sub-group which meets our needs without at the same time imposing on us other conditions with which we strongly disagree. Also, in the modern world where institutions are so interconnected and ideas from everywhere are carried daily by the media to virtually every human being, it is difficult for sub-groups to escape the influence of general social structures. Accordingly, even those who do belong to sub-communities must for their own protection try to influence the nature of the wider society.

Clearly, then, a major means of adult values education is through action to improve bad social structures (or maintain good ones). Indeed, programs of values education which don't include a social action component can expect only limited success. The traditional conception is that we learn better values — at university, at the temple, through therapy, through self-help books, or whatever — and then proceed to change how we live. But to a large degree the converse is true: our values are changed through changes in how we live, which to a considerable extent is dictated by society. Individual study and reflection is important. But we need an interactive process in which societal change leads to individual insight and vice versa.

One of the problems of a purely individual and intellectual approach is that new values are difficult to envisage in the abstract. Prior to societal change, we lack detailed insight into a different way of life and how it would work. Indeed we can't know for certain *that* it would work. We can say in general terms what is needed — for example, a non-sexist life-style — but unless we are participating in a societal process of establishing non-sexist structures at home, in the workplace, and elsewhere, how can we know what a non-sexist way of life would look like, or be sure it would be a good thing? The general ideal of gender equality is (I think) an important one to disseminate and as far as possible "teach" people. But learning of this abstract, verbal kind is just part of learning non-sexist values.

"Instruction" in Values

While adults learn values in more ways than we have commonly recognized, the age-old approach of direct instruction still has a place. (And we should note that this approach can now be implemented in many non-traditional ways: through TV, radio, newspapers, magazines, popular books, videos, computerized information retrieval systems, and so on.)

We saw in Part 1 that values have a major objective component, and hence factual information is highly relevant in making value choices. People have a strong interest in the outcomes of their behavior, and will adjust their values and actions in the light of information about the consequences of behavior. Much of this information can be made available through instruction.

As we noted in Chapter 8, according to David Gauthier, our basic moral policies and dispositions change very little after middle childhood. From then on, a chief means of moral education is that of straightforwardly explaining the consequences of various actions, thus enabling us to give appropriate expression to our policies and dispositions. One might add that instruction can help us see not only the consequences of familiar types of actions, but also new and better ways of acting to achieve our values. We may be aware of harmful effects of our behavior — for example, on the environment — but not be able to see any alternative.

Instruction (through various media) can also introduce people to new ways of viewing reality. This has been the impact, for example, of knowledge of Eastern religious and philosophical perspectives in the West in recent times. Concepts of "non-violence," "going with the flow," and "the totality of things" have helped counter Western images of continuous struggle, humans "over against" nature, and God "out there." The rather straightforward presentation of information about other world views, then, has helped lead to key value shifts toward a more adequate personal, global, and ecological outlook.

In the past, of course, the instructional mode has often been abused. Through it, people have had their time wasted and have been brow-beaten, indoctrinated, or simply bored. It's for this reason that, in the title of this section, I put the word "instruction" in quotation marks. What is needed is a new type of "instruction," of a kind we will consider more fully in Chapters 13 and 14. However, the fact remains that, properly understood, instruction is one of the major ways in which adults learn values.

CHAPTER 13

Approaches to Values Education

In this chapter, I will look at various historical and contemporary approaches to values education. While my interest will be in their suitability for adults, it should be noted that to date some of them have been used mainly with children. Also, while I will speak of them in relation to *values* education, some have previously been used more in the sub-field of *moral* education.

In the space available, I can discuss only some aspects of the approaches. Much more extensive treatments of many of them may be found elsewhere.[1] However, even a brief introduction is obviously better than none; and I will try to focus on elements which are particularly

1. See, for example, R. Hersh, J. Miller, and G. Fielding, *Models of Moral Education: An Appraisal* (New York: Longman, 1980); and J. Elias, *Moral Education: Secular and Religious* (Malabar, Florida: Krieger Publ. Co., 1989).

important for arriving at a sound comprehensive approach to adult values education.

While I will be rather critical of many of the approaches, I believe each has something to offer which deserves to be incorporated into a broader approach. My main criticism will be not that the approaches are without merit but that each in its own way is too narrow and needs to have many other components added to it.

Socialization

An ancient method of fostering values in people is simply to immerse them in a community, society, or culture. In this way, through largely unconscious means, people "pick up" values from their socio-cultural environment. This happens to all of us and to a large extent makes us what we are, for good and ill. I discussed "social learning" in Chapter 12. Here I wish to discuss the same phenomenon as a more deliberate, *educational* process.

The absorption of values from society isn't only inescapable; in many ways it is desirable and is to be promoted. Richard Peters has argued convincingly that we must to a degree be "initiated" into a social and intellectual tradition before we can reflectively evaluate it: "individual inventiveness can only emerge against a background of a public tradition which has provided both the milieu for problems and the procedures for tackling them."[2] Richard Hare has observed that, if morality is to be possible at all, some kind of foundation must be laid in early childhood. He says, for example, that children have to realize that what is wrong for others to do to them is wrong for them to do to others. And "unless *some* non-rational methods are used, it's unlikely that all our

2. R. Peters, *Ethics and Education* (London: Allen and Unwin, 1966), p. 57.

children will come to absorb this principle as deeply as we could wish; and to that extent less of their thinking about action will be moral thinking, and their actions will show this."[3]

A great champion of socialization in the modern era was Emile Durkheim. In his celebrated book *Moral Education*, Durkheim argues that in order to survive and prosper a society must develop a sound morality and ensure, through socialization, that it is embraced by its members. He talks of the importance of affective learning, saying that "since we are and always will be sensate as well as rational human beings," complete freedom of choice of values is an impossible ideal.[4] And he describes the task of moral education as that of fostering respect for rules ("discipline"), a positive regard for certain social groups ("attachment"), and "enlightened allegiance" or "informed consent" to societal authority ("autonomy").

It should be noted, however, that Durkheim was not the arch socializer, the extreme exponent of conformity he is sometimes thought to be. As the terms "informed consent" and "autonomy" suggest, Durkheim believed that respect for and allegiance to the society's morality must be based in part on individual understanding and judgment. "To teach morality," he says, "is neither to preach nor to indoctrinate; it's to explain." We must "help (children) understand the reasons for the rules (they) should abide by," otherwise "we would be condemning (them) to an incomplete and inferior morality" (pp. 120-21). Further, Durkheim doesn't believe that societal maintenance should ride roughshod over the needs of the

3. R. Hare, "Adolescents into Adults," in *Aims in Education: The Philosophic Approach*, ed. T.H.B. Hollins (Manchester: Manchester University Press, 1964), pp. 63-64.
4. E. Durkheim, *Moral Education: A Study in the Theory and Application of the Sociology of Education* (New York: Free Press, 1961; originally 1925), pp. 113-14.

individual: "If (an institution) does violence to human nature, however socially useful it may be, it will never be born, much less persist since it can't take root in the conscience" (p. 38). Durkheim sees the relationship between the individual and society as dialectical. Individuals participate in society's "science of moral matters" and thereby influence the development of the morality of the society which in turn influences them (pp. 119-20).

It might be thought that socialization has little relevance to adult education since it takes place in childhood. However, as John Elias points out in *Moral Education: Secular and Religious,* social scientists in recent years have used the concept of socialization "to explain changes in adult life. In general terms they have attempted to determine how adults develop throughout the life span. Socialization takes place because of the demands of others, role or status change (marriage, parenthood, widowhood, retirement), occupational entry or shift, developmental changes in family . . . ." Thus, new socialization of these kinds occurs during adulthood, together with re-socialization with respect to childhood moral values.[5]

Socialization, then, is an important means of values learning, in adulthood as well as childhood. The main problem with it is that it doesn't involve sufficient critical reflection; indeed, in a strict sense it is often not *education* at all. So, to see it as the whole of values education, to define education *as* socialization (as some educational theorists, remarkably, have done) is as great a mistake as to ignore its role. Even from early childhood, and certainly from early adulthood, people must be encouraged and helped to *assess the appropriateness* of the values which have been, are being, or will be pressed upon them

5. *Moral Education: Secular and Religious,* p. 124.

through social processes. This critical activity takes them beyond socialization.

Habituation

According to Aristotle, becoming a virtuous person takes practice. Through practice, we *clarify what is right,* what is the "golden mean" in different types of situation; and we *strengthen our disposition to do what is right.* "Moral Excellence . . . denotes a settled habit, formed by a course of actions under rule and discipline . . . so that the virtuous (person), without internal conflict, wills actions that hit the happy mean in their effects."[6]

We acquire good habits in part through our own efforts. By deliberately making sound moral choices, we build up our moral insight and dispositions, our moral character.[7] However, other people also have an important role to play in leading us to act appropriately and hence develop habits. This they do through reward, punishment, "discipline," exhortation, law making, and a variety of other means.[8]

While habituation is an important component in moral development, its significance has sometimes been exaggerated. Right action in a situation is only partly the result of previously established habits. Behavior is also influenced by current desires, external influences, and new insights (as Aristotle acknowledges).

It is dangerous, then, to think that habit formation alone is important in learning values. It may lead us to rely on *forcing* people — our children, for example, or our employees — to behave in certain ways in the hope that

6. H. Sidgwick, *Outlines of the History of Ethics,* 6th ed. (London: Macmillan, 1931), p. 59.
7. Aristotle, *Ethics,* edited and translated by John Warrington, (London: Dent, Everyman's Library, 1963), p. 32.
8. *Ibid.,* pp. 28-29.

this will make them better. In fact, enforced behavior often doesn't become permanent; on the contrary, it may be vigorously rejected later. And the process of forcing people to do things can have many negative side-effects. Accordingly, it is important to supplement habituation, as a method of values education, with a wide variety of other techniques.

Liberal Education

In Western countries in the modern era it has been thought good for young adults to study the "liberal arts," that is, subjects such as literature, philosophy, languages, and history, as distinct from professional or technical subjects. It has been assumed that, among other things, this will have a broadening and humanizing effect, tending to make people reasonable, tolerant, and fair. Similar assumptions have been made about continued exposure to literature, theatre, music, and the like in later life. It came as a surprise, for example, that those who took part in genocide during World War II included many liberally educated, "cultured" people. How could one, it was asked, be an enthusiastic death camp supervisor by day and return to Schiller, Goethe, and Beethoven in the evening?

But the scope of the liberal arts is in fact more limited than many educators have realized. High literature, for example, can certainly give us deeper insight into the human condition, but often it deals mainly with the aspirations and problems of a particular race and class. And even within that scope, its interests are usually not so much to reform as to reveal and delight. History, too, is pursued by many historians as if it were a search for "the facts" rather than an exploration of values; and insofar as it deals with value issues it has often, notoriously, been used to glorify and justify the exploits of a particular sub-group of a particular society. Philosophy, similarly, contains many sub-fields which make no claim to deal extensively with values; and in recent years many of these sub-fields — philosophy of language, philosophy of mind, philosophy of science, for example — have been central to the study of philosophy.

While the systematic pursuit of insights into human life is obviously essential for value inquiry, some insights are more relevant than others. An education in values must identify those facts and ideas which bear on pressing value issues, and organize them so that their implications are clear. Even when liberal education explores ideas which are *potentially* significant for value questions, it often doesn't go on to show how they are significant. Critical value inquiry *could*, of course, have been a major sub-field within liberal education, and a major dimension of the other liberal arts subjects. Perhaps we should work for a re-definition of liberal arts which requires this. But in the past this is simply not how liberal education has been understood. We may conclude, then, that liberal education as traditionally defined is an important but not sufficient factor in value development. It needs to be complemented by many other activities.

Direct Instruction in Values

Socialization and habituation have the shortcoming that they don't involve enough reflection and conscious choice on the part of learners. Liberal education has the limitation that it often doesn't directly address value issues. Both these problems can be reduced by the centuries-old method of direct teaching in values, in which values topics are openly and systematically considered.

The occasional courses in ethics or values in schools, colleges, universities, religious centres, community centres, and so on, provide examples of this type of instruction. Separate courses, however, aren't essential to the approach. Values teaching can be integrated into courses on other topics such as literature, science, and medicine, and into practical training programs on, for example, parenting and financial planning.

At present, the explicit teaching of ethics or values, insofar as it occurs at all, is often too "academic." Everyday value questions are largely ignored, while whole courses are devoted to one or two obscure historical texts, or to detailed technical analysis of a few concepts and arguments. However, values teaching need not be like this. It can be clear, interesting, comprehensive, full of everyday examples, and of practical value.

In my view, perhaps the greatest single advance in values education could be brought about by increased values teaching. It's a scandal that our systems of formal education are filled with instruction in almost everything but basic life questions. Educational systems may be inefficient, but they have an impact. People learn much about literature, history, science, and mathematics in schools and universities. Why not values?

Not just any type of values instruction will do, however. It must be clear, relevant, and comprehensive, as we have noted. Further, it should be "dialogical" (as we will discuss in Chapter 14), with instructors listening to and learning from students as well as vice versa. Teachers and students must learn together. While instructors should feel free to advocate certain values, students should have the same freedom, and everyone's views should be open to modification through interaction. There should not be pre-established answers which are simply transmitted to students.

In ideal values instruction, then, a large proportion of the "teaching" is done by the learners, who instruct each other and their "teacher." The main point of values instruction, therefore, isn't that one person tells other people what to value, but rather that there is explicit, systematic, joint inquiry into value matters. Hence, the notion that values instruction should be avoided because it's inevitably authoritarian and indoctrinating can be rejected. It's true that teachers often have a direct influence on students, even when they try not to. But students also have a direct impact on each other and on teachers. And in life in general, as we saw in Chapter 12, people constantly influence each other directly, because we are social beings. The occurrence of this phenomenon isn't an argument for avoiding explicit, co-ordinated study of values.

While instruction in values (as I have described it) is legitimate, however, it's not the only means of teaching and learning values. It must be supplemented by many other approaches. Its main limitation is that the instructional setting is nearly always artificially cut off from the rest of life. This limitation has sometimes been exaggerated: there is much to be said for periods of withdrawal from the real world in order to reflect. But the limitation remains: in classrooms, places of worship, or conference centres we are often carried away by theories and extreme ideals and forget what real life is like, insofar as we knew. We need to move constantly back and forth between reflection and absorption, instruction and "learning from life."

Therapeutic Approaches

Adults educators often advocate using, in values learning, methods drawn from the psychological health field. Also, most psychological counsellors and analysts engage in values education as *part* of a program of therapy for adults, whether they are aware of doing so or not. Eric Berne's transactional analysis, for example, has been used to help adults understand the damaging "games people play" in their relationships and develop more appropriate, "adult" ways of interacting. Carl Rogers's "non-directive therapy" has been seen by Rogers himself and by many educators as offering techniques for enabling adults to cast off the overlay of "introjected" values acquired during childhood and adolescence and return to more natural and healthy outlooks and life patterns. Herbert Freudenberger's ways of conceptualizing and treating "burnout" in his clients have been seen as having broad implications for adults in general. And Viktor Frankl's "logotherapy" has been hailed as offering important insights into how all human beings should respond to the difficulties of modern life.

While therapeutic approaches to values learning have something to offer, we need to remind ourselves of their limitations and their origins in the treatment of mentally "ill" patients. The breadth of the learning involved in each case is often not sufficient for a full values education program; and the methods used are often stronger than is justified for "normal" adults. Psychotherapy clients typically have more stubborn blocks and more extreme symptoms than the general population. Also, psychotherapy professionals, following Freud, often tend to see the problems of their clients as due to pre-adult experiences and the solutions as involving primarily a psychological journey back to those experiences in order to "repair" earlier damage. This bias toward the past, and toward radical personal change, is perhaps not justified even for psychiatric clients and is certainly often inappropriate for the adult population as a whole. (We saw some of the limitations of a therapeutic approach in our discussion of David Smail's views in Chapter 12.)

Perhaps the main shortcoming of therapeutic approaches (from a values education point of view) is that they have tended to overlook the complex *theoretical* task involved in developing sound values. It's often assumed that the right and the good is known, and what is needed is a psychological technique to establish the appropriate value in the person or to clear away "blocks," "scripts," or the like which are preventing a value from emerging or being expressed. But as we have noted before, much of the problem is *knowing* what is right and why; and when people behave inappropriately it's often not because they have psychological hang-ups but because they don't know what is right (and neither does anyone else). Therapeutic work, then, needs to be accompanied by other approaches which try to find answers to value questions.

With qualifications such as these, however, values educators are well advised to look to psychotherapy for insights and techniques. Mental illness is usually an extreme form of a malady which is widespread in society and brings suffering and a measure of disability to virtually all people. As Smail says:

> I do not believe that the kind of people who consult psychotherapists are particularly unusual, nor that the kinds of "problems" they have are any different from anyone else's. Differences . . . are matters of degree rather than kind.[9]

Further, some psychotherapists have been quicker than others to realize that a major contribution to people's problems is an inadequate value system, and have led the way in attempting to foster more appropriate values. Some therapists have been conservative and authoritarian in value matters, but others have worked hard to free people from disabling value "hang-ups" and taboos.

The Cognitive Developmental Approach

This approach has its roots in the work of Jean Piaget, who reacted against what he saw as an overly authoritarian, unreflective emphasis in Durkheim's position. According to Piaget, the child's early authority-oriented (heteronomous) morality represents a stage of "disequilib-

9. D. Smail, *Taking Care: An Alternative to Therapy* (London: Dent, 1987), p. 79.

rium," and children need to pass steadily on to a co-operative, reflective (autonomous) morality.

While rejecting socialization in Durkheim's sense, however, Piaget attaches a great deal of importance to *social interaction* of children, especially with each other, as a means of moral development. In the context of criticizing Durkheim's proposal "to impress upon the child a fully worked-out system of discipline," Piaget claims that "the social life of children amongst themselves is sufficiently developed to give rise to a discipline infinitely nearer to that inner submission which is the mark of adult morality."[10] Piaget is confident that, given this social interaction, children will progress because their "own taste for active research and (their) desire for cooperation suffice to ensure a normal intellectual development." Children will grow morally through a largely natural process of "individual experimentation" on the one hand and "reflection carried out in common" on the other (p. 412). Instruction has a place, notably to provide children with relevant scientific information. But it mustn't be used to impose "the dictates of adult society": the adult teacher must be "a collaborator and not a master" (pp. 374-75, 412).

We find in Lawrence Kohlberg key elements of the theory of moral development earlier presented by Piaget: The idea of children moving by a relatively natural process from an earlier authority-oriented level of morality to a later autonomous level. The idea of children, as "young moral philosophers," needing social experience but playing a major role in the development of their own thinking about morality. The strong rejection of socialization as an appropriate approach to moral education on the twofold ground that it's authoritarian and unreflec-

10. J. Piaget, *The Moral Judgment of the Child*, transl. Marjorie Gabin (London: Routledge and Kegan Paul, 1932), pp. 411-12.

tive. The notion of the teacher as someone who facilitates moral development, stimulating growth not by telling students the right answers but by confronting them with moral dilemmas, alternative modes of reasoning, and structured situations which help them see the inherent instability and logical inadequacy of their earlier moral ideas and as a result move on to more stable and adequate ideas.

Beyond Piaget, Kohlberg elaborates moral development theory very considerably, identifying in great detail the stages through which children are thought to go. He develops the dilemma discussion method, suggesting how dilemmas that would not normally arise may be brought into the classroom, and outlining how they might be used in an attempt to move students from one stage to another. He establishes detailed procedures for identifying, characterizing, and measuring the moral stage and type of children; and refines the theory and practice of establishing "just schools" within which children can develop morally. Finally, he expounds at length a theory of morality — to which justice, reciprocity, and respect for persons are central — and describes how children's conception of morality progressively approaches "true" morality as they become morally more mature.

As we saw in Chapter 7, Kohlberg also goes beyond Piaget in extending moral development theory into adulthood. He maintains that people are rarely "autonomous" by their early twenties and so still have a considerable amount of moral learning to do (in this he follows Erikson rather than Piaget). And he sees the methods advocated for stimulating moral development in children as applicable to adults as well (although often in less formal settings).

In many ways, the strengths of the cognitive developmental approach are also its weaknesses. It rightly points to the need for critical reflection on values; but goes too far, to an almost exclusively cognitive approach. It's optimistic about the powers of people, as amateur "moral philosophers," to learn naturally through everyday experience and conversation; but underemphasizes the need for systematic study of values linked to formal academic traditions. It stresses the autonomy of the individual; but in doing so downplays the influence which friends, teachers, institutions, and society inevitably have on people's values, for good and ill. Thus, there is much to learn from the approach, but we must be aware of its gaps and excesses.

Perhaps the main weakness of the approach is its assumption that older people are on average morally wiser than younger people. We noted in Chapter 7 how this can spoil relationships across generations and in particular the relationship between "teacher" and "taught." It threatens the principle put forward earlier that "teachers and students should learn together." Interestingly, undermining this principle was not the intention of Piaget, who saw young people achieving moral autonomy before they became adults, and insisted that a teacher should be "a collaborator and not a master." Kohlberg attempts to retain this aspect of Piaget's approach by proposing that teachers should not give answers but rather "stimulate natural development." However, once it's accepted that older is wiser, genuine respect and dialogue between generations becomes difficult, no matter how much the older person *tries* to be non-judgmental. A negative assessment of younger people by older people is built into the very structure of the present-day cognitive developmental approach.

The Value Analysis and Reasoning Skills Approach

Direct instruction in values is often opposed on the ground that it is *necessarily* indoctrinating. (As noted earlier, I don't believe this is so.) In the sixties and seventies a number of values educators sought to avoid indoctrination by teaching analytic schemes and reasoning skills rather than value content. Among those offering an approach of this kind were Fred Newmann and Donald Oliver,[11] James Shaver,[12] Jerrold Coombs and Milton Mieux,[13] and Michael Scriven.[14] Each of these writers, in slightly varying ways, proposed a threefold curriculum for the study of values: (a) study of relevant factual information; (b) study of basic theory of values, including an analytic scheme for identifying the elements in a value problem; and (c) acquisition of reasoning skills for the satisfactory resolution of issues. Often a heavy emphasis was placed on the discussion of historical cases or hypothetical dilemmas as a means of illustrating theoretical concepts and honing reasoning skills. It was proposed that the teacher should maintain the stance of a neutral discussion organizer and information source, or at times a Socratic devil's advocate. Only occasionally, on an especially serious matter (for example, racism), might a teacher come down on a particular side.

The main problem with this approach is that it assumes value neutrality is possible when in fact it's not. Any theory of values, conceptual scheme, or set of reasoning skills has underlying it a system of substantive values. If this isn't acknowledged, a number of unfortunate consequences follow.

11. F. Newmann and D. Oliver, *Clarifying Public Controversy* (Boston: Little, Brown, 1970).
12. J. Shaver and W. Strong, *Facing Value Decisions* (Belmont, CA: Wadsworth, 1976).
13. J. Coombs and M. Mieux, "Teaching Strategies for Value Analysis," in *Values Education*, ed. L. Metcalf (Washington, D.C.: National Council for Social Studies, 1971).
14. M. Scriven, "Cognitive Moral Education," *Kappan*, **56**, 10 (1975), 689-94.

First, if the value assumptions of an approach aren't acknowledged, they aren't evaluated and are simply absorbed by students as they are exposed to the approach. Thus the attempt to *avoid* indoctrination leads directly *to* indoctrination. Shaver, for example, "focuses on the need to teach the specific analytic skills he deems essential to democratic citizenship."[15] But by teaching these skills and avoiding discussion of substantive values underlying the Western democratic model (of the American kind Shaver has in mind), this approach imposes these values on students.

Second, attempting to be neutral when we can't be leads to an unproductive game in which students attempt to guess the teacher's values. Scriven was once asked what he would do if, after extensive discussion, his students didn't conclude that capital punishment was wrong. He replied: "We would keep on discussing." Obviously, with such an approach, students would quickly learn that they have got the "right" answer when the teacher allows them to stop discussing. It would seem to be more productive for the teacher's view to be on the table, along with a number of others, so students may evaluate it (and the teacher re-evaluate it, in light of students' comments).

Third, trying to be neutral can lead to boredom for both students and teachers. Both must be able to reveal their value beliefs and feel the excitement of making progress in improving them. The study of facts, concepts, and rules of reasoning in isolation from the attempt to resolve pressing and personally relevant life issues will be experienced as both uninteresting and pointless.

Finally, trying to be neutral leads to neglect of value content, thus leaving students without help in dealing

15. R. Hersh, J. Miller, and G. Fielding, *Models of Moral Education* (New York: Longman, 1980), p. 27.

with concrete problems. It's not sufficient to equip people with an analytic scheme and a set of reasoning skills and send them out into the world to survive as rugged individuals. They need the assistance of teachers and co-learners in establishing their substantive value system and confronting particular issues.

Of course, it's important to learn about the nature of values and acquire problem-solving skills. But much else must be done *at the same time*. We have here yet another example of the need to use several approaches at once in values education, instead of relying on one, narrow approach.

Values Clarification

Values clarification is associated especially with the names of Louis Raths and Sidney Simon.[16] It's widely talked about in adult education circles, and the term "values clarification" is sometimes used as a substitute for "values education." It's important to note, however, that VC (as it's often called) is just one values education approach among many, with distinctive assumptions and techniques.

VC is perhaps best known for its group activities, often used as warm-ups at the beginning of workshops or to stimulate thought about a value issue prior to discussion. The handbook *Values Clarification* by Simon et al. describes seventy-nine such activities, including infamous ones such as "The Fall-Out Shelter" and "Cave-in Simulation" and more innocuous ones such as "Personal Coat of Arms" and "Epitaph." We should recognize, however, that a rationale lies behind these diverse activities. Together they are intended to encourage:

16. See, for example, L. Raths, M. Harmin, and S. Simon, *Values and Teaching*, rev. ed. (Columbus, Ohio: Merrill, 1978; 1st ed. 1966); and S. Simon et al., *Values Clarification* (New York: Hart, 1972).

- Choosing: (1) freely
  (2) from alternatives
  (3) after thoughtful consideration of the consequences of each alternative
- Prizing: (4) cherishing, being happy with the choice
  (5) enough to be willing to affirm the choice to others
- Acting: (6) or doing something with the choice
  (7) repeatedly, in some pattern of life[17]

Advocates of VC believe that our traditional approaches to values education are both too abstract and too judgmental, and the proposed activities are designed to overcome these weaknesses. The activities focus largely on personal life concerns, and are meant to develop learners who are expressive, confident, and active valuers. Underlying VC is considerable optimism about the desires and values people actually have as distinct from ones others think they should have. Hence the name "values clarification": the main object is to help people clarify their values (and feel good about them and act on them) rather than change them. But there is provision for self-initiated change, after reflection on the nature and consequences of one's values.

VC has much to offer. Most of its activities are enjoyable and "work well." Its emphasis on self-esteem is unusual and important. And its optimism about ordinary human desires and values is largely sound, tying in with the notion, explored in Chapter 2, that natural "basic values" must form the main foundation of a value system.

However, some shortcomings should be noted. To begin with, falling broadly within the "liberal" tradition, VC exaggerates the extent to which people can make free,

17. *Values and Teaching*, p. 28.

individual choices. In practice, as social beings, we are very much influenced by the values of our society and the people around us. This weakness of the approach has become apparent in some VC activity groups where the effect of group pressure on response and choice has proved to be greater than expected (for example, in the "Cave-in Simulation" activity, where group members often gang-up on each other, or apply cultural stereotypes in deciding who is a worthwhile person). VC hasn't recognized sufficiently the need to counterbalance these forces.

Further, the completely accepting, uncritical approach to people's values advocated by VC is too extreme. People's *basic* desire for survival, happiness, companionship, and so on is legitimate; but at more *specific* levels we often make mistakes in value matters (as we saw in Chapter 2), and attention should sometimes be drawn to such mistakes (for example, damaging the environment, consuming too much, working too hard, neglecting our health, neglecting our relationships).

VC advocates believe that unconditional support of learners' values is necessary to strengthen their self-esteem. But there are several problems here. First, if people have unsound values, the resulting harm (to themselves and others) may outweigh the benefits of increased self-esteem. Second, if people have unsound values, an artificial self-esteem created in the classroom or at the week-end workshop will soon dissipate in the real world, as they and others recognize the mistakes they are making. And third, helping people see weaknesses (as well as strengths) in their value system need not undermine their self-esteem, so long as an adequate explanation is given of the social and cultural origins of these problems (something which VC doesn't offer). VC exponents are right in maintaining that guilt reduction is crucial in value development. However, this is often best achieved not by overlooking problems but rather by clarifying where the causes lie.

The final and crucial shortcoming of the VC approach is that it deals only with process and ignores value content. (In this respect it's like the value analysis and reasoning skills approach.) The exhortation to weigh the consequences of alternative values and then be positive about the choices made is quite inadequate. People need a complex view of what is valuable in life on the basis of which they can make sound choices; and because VC has no explicit opinions on this, leaving it up to the individual, it has no substantive insights to offer.

Perspective Transformation

Advocated by adult education theorist Jack Mezirow, perspective transformation isn't strictly a values education approach since it's concerned with one's total world view or "meaning perspective." However, a meaning perspective includes values as a major component, and accordingly many of the points Mezirow makes about perspective transformation are directly relevant to values education.

According to Mezirow, we adult educators have largely neglected the *fundamentals* of life and learning, making "the egregious error" of defining our function "solely as one of fostering behavior change and (acting) as though we believe our principal tasks are to do needs assessment surveys, to communicate ideas, and to design exercises to develop specific knowledge, skills, or attitudes for prescribed behavior change."[18] The problem here is that "not only does this effort often become indoctrination to engineer consent, but it frequently

18. J. Mezirow, "Perspective Transformation," *Adult Education*, **28**, 2 (1978), 107.

addresses the wrong reality to begin with" (p. 107). What adult educators should do in addition — indeed *primarily* — is help people become aware of and change as necessary "the cultural and psychological assumptions that have influenced the way we see ourselves and our relationships and the way we pattern our lives," that is, our "meaning perspectives" (p. 101).

In Mezirow's view, "meaning perspectives are, for the most part, uncritically acquired in childhood through the process of socialization, often in the context of an emotionally charged relationship with parents, teachers, or other mentors."[19] Perspective *transformation*, by contrast, tends to be more an adult phenomenon. One of the main ways in which it's triggered is through "certain challenges or dilemmas of adult life that can't be resolved by the usual way we handle problems. Examples are found in what popular writers have referred to as 'life crises.' The sudden loss of a mate or a job, a change of residence, graduation from college, betrayal or rejection . . . ."[20] However, the less dramatic procedures of adult education can also be used "to precipitate, facilitate, and reinforce perspective transformation as well as to implement resulting action plans." Indeed, according to Mezirow, "there is no higher priority for adult education than to develop its potentialities for perspective transformation" (p. 109).

In elaborating his approach, especially in his more recent writings, Mezirow has drawn heavily on the ideas of contemporary German philosopher Jürgen Habermas. Following Habermas, he distinguishes between "instrumental learning," which is concerned with empirical and technical knowledge and ways of controlling and manipu-

19. J. Mezirow and Associates, *Fostering Critical Reflection in Adulthood* (San Francisco: Jossey-Bass, 1990), p. 3.
20. "Perspective Transformation," p. 101.

lating one's environment, and "communicative learning," which is concerned with "hermeneutics" or interpretation and explanation of experience. Closely related to communicative learning is "emancipatory learning," which involves fundamental *critique* of the interpretive systems understood through communicative learning. Perspective transformation, according to Mezirow, occurs largely in the realm of and as a result of communicative and emancipatory learning.[21] It's this type of learning which has been so unfortunately neglected by adult education.

Again following Habermas, Mezirow discusses at length the constraints or "distortions" which commonly affect our meaning perspectives, including our values. Perspective transformation is achieved "through a critically reflective assessment of *epistemic, socio-cultural,* and *psychic* distortions acquired through the process of introjection, the uncritical acceptance of another's values."[22] *Epistemic distortions* include the presupposition that there are final (as distinct from provisional) answers, and the belief that social and cultural phenomena are immutable, beyond human control (the problem of "reification"). *Socio-cultural distortions* include a range of negative stereotypes, inappropriate social norms, and harmful ideologies. And *psychic distortions* are ideationally-based inhibitions or blocks, "presuppositions generating unwarranted anxiety that impedes taking action" (pp. 15-17). In Mezirow's view, adult education has largely overlooked culturally based problems of these kinds and left learners with virtually no means of dealing with them.

In my view, the perspective transformation approach, including the contribution of other writers to which Mezirow refers (for example, Habermas, Freire, Kuhn),

21. J. Mezirow, "A Critical Theory of Adult Learning and Education," *Adult Education*, **32**, 1 (Fall, 1981), 4-6.
22. *Fostering Critical Reflection in Adulthood*, p. 14.

has the potential to strengthen adult values education significantly. Of particular note is its focus on: (a) fundamental reflection on life's meaning and goals; (b) analysis of the socio-cultural origins of many of our problems, for which in the past individuals have been held accountable; (c) the ideational as distinct from purely psychological origins of many problems; (d) the importance of dialogue as opposed to indoctrination in acquiring values; and (e) the importance of action as a means of validating meanings and consolidating learning. These emphases provide a necessary corrective to many traditional and contemporary approaches to values education.

However, it's important to be aware of the shortcomings of Mezirow's approach, arising especially from his reliance on Habermas. According to Mezirow, when we are in the communicative mode of inquiry, which has to do with values, ideals, moral issues, and so on, we must rely on social consensus as the means of validation. This position presents two major difficulties: (a) it assumes a sharp dichotomy between values and "instrumental" or "strategic" matters; and (b) it implies that values can't be objectively validated. Further, having taken this stand, Mezirow (like Habermas) can only offer a procedural ethic, lacking in substantive guidance. We are exhorted to reflect and dialogue, and given a set of conditions of rational discussion, but are offered very few ideas about what is good and important in life.[23] A parallel may be drawn here with values clarification, which offers a method without content. Perspective transformation represents an advance over VC because it recognizes the constraints and opportunities of the wider socio-cultural context. But the absence of a substantive value theory remains a major drawback. In order to

23. J. Mezirow, *Transformative Dimensions of Adult Learning* (San Francisco: Jossey-Bass, 1991), pp. 75-78.

appropriate Mezirow's insights, then, we must incorporate them into a broader approach to values education.

Self-Directed Learning

Self-directed learning, like perspective transformation, isn't specifically an approach to values education. However, it's seen by its advocates as a key to development in personal areas, including values. Allen Tough, for example, sees it as an appropriate method "within the *human growth* cluster of subject matter" in general, and in particular as applicable in "efforts to *reform or rehabilitate* certain individuals."[24]

Advocates of self-directed learning point out that people can and do learn a great deal through their own efforts; and also that learning directed by others is often ineffective, either because the learner isn't vitally engaged, or because the program of study isn't sufficiently focussed on what the learner needs. There are exceptions, of course. But learning is usually at its most effective when learners are consciously managing their own education and on guard against the pitfalls of formal and large-group education. This applies especially to values, where personal choice is crucial and where there is a long history of imposition through indoctrination.

The term "self-directed learning" is ambiguous. It may mean learning carried out by the individual, in relative isolation from other people (for example, where I teach myself to play the piano); or learning deliberately planned by individuals to meet their needs, but sometimes relying on the services of others (for example, I may take strong initiative in learning to play the piano, but go to one or

24. A. Tough, *The Adult's Learning Projects* (Toronto: OISE Press, 1971), pp. 168-69. His italics.

more teachers for lesson series of varying duration; I may even take group lessons).

K. P. Cross in *Adults as Learners* defines self-directed learning as "deliberate learning in which the person's primary intention is to 'gain certain definite knowledge or skills'."[25] She goes on:

> Researchers identified with self-directed learning (Tough, Penland, and Coolican) usually include formal learning and class work in their analyses of learning projects, but when the object of study is *all* of the deliberate learning efforts of the individual, organized group learning constitutes a small portion of the total of effort. (p. 187)

Expressing her concern at the ambiguity of the term, Cross says:

> It would be helpful if the literature on self-directed learning contained more case studies, so that we had a better feel for what kind of learning we are actually talking about. (p. 187)

Despite the ambiguity of the term, we may say that advocacy of self-directed learning signals a high (if not exclusive) emphasis on the role of the *individual*. And herein lies a danger. Contemporary Western culture is already too individualistic in many ways, and we don't need unqualified exhortations to become more so. It is true that — as I have argued in this book — the moral right of individuals to look after their own well-being has often been overlooked. However, we must look after the well-being of others to a degree also; and besides, even in learning to promote our own well-being we must work *with others* to a large extent. Further, the self-directed

25. K. Cross, *Adults as Learners* (San Francisco: Jossey-Bass, 1981), pp. 186-87.

learning movement runs the risk of overestimating the extent to which individuals can change themselves, without parallel changes in society.

Jack Mezirow, as we saw in the previous section, has made an important contribution by emphasizing the need for a cultural and societal perspective in adult education. However, somewhat inconsistently, he places a great deal of emphasis on self-direction. He states that helping adults "assume responsibility for decision making is the essence of education," and adult educators are committed to "the concept of learner self-directedness as both the means and the end of education."[26] He defines andragogy (by contrast with pedagogy) as "an organized and sustained effort to assist adults to learn *in a way that enhances their capability to function as self-directed learners*."[27] And he maintains that developmental research has shown self-directed learning to be "the mode of learning characteristic of adulthood" (by contrast with childhood).[28]

There are several problems here. In emphasizing so strongly the difference between adults' and children's styles of learning, Mezirow shows a heavy dependence on developmentalism of the kind rejected in Chapter 7, above. Interestingly, in doing so, Mezirow is at variance with his own suggestion (in a later work) that children are capable of the type of "communicative competence" he advocates fostering in adults.[29] Moreover, in maintaining his position he goes beyond key developmentalists such as Piaget, who sees autonomy emerging at least by the early teens, and Kohlberg, who describes children as "young moral philosophers" with considerable capacity

26. "A Critical Theory of Adult Learning and Education," p. 20.
27. *Ibid.*, p. 21. His italics.
28. *Ibid.*
29. *Fostering Critical Reflection in Adulthood*, p. 359.

for developing moral ideas on their own in light of their everyday experience.

But even more importantly, Mezirow's statements on self-direction appear to contradict his own general view that individuals are greatly influenced by the ideologies and practices of the society to which they belong. Perhaps he believes that, while having been so influenced up to this point, adults can as a result of certain life experiences and educational programs learn to throw off their old outlooks single-handedly and in the future escape the influence of society on their judgments and choices. However, apart from being rather implausible, this position isn't at all the one adopted by Habermas and Freire (on whom Mezirow draws heavily) who stress the *continued* influence of society on the individual and hence the need for societal (as well as individual) change.

The main point then is that, while self-direction has an important place in values learning, its role should not be exaggerated. In some respects we do need to encourage people (both adults *and* children, by the way) to exercise more initiative, to take more control of their lives, to become more reflective about where they are going and how (as we saw in Chapter 10). But also we need to emphasize (as Mezirow does elsewhere) that humans are inevitably social beings, living in a web of relationships, influenced by structures and practices of society, who must work with and through their community in order to achieve well-being.

Trying to Be Comprehensive

About ten years ago I presented a paper entitled "Moral Education: A Comprehensive Approach" at an international conference on values and education in Québec. I noted there, as I have here, that many conceptions of moral education have the weakness of being too narrow; and then proceeded to give what I thought was a comprehensive account of moral (and values) education. The paper was well received: we educators, like baseball players, like the feeling that all the bases have been covered. However, looking back I realize how much I had unwittingly omitted. While we will never succeed completely, we must constantly try to be comprehensive. Value issues are extremely complex, and if we settle for a narrower outlook important considerations will be left out. In this final part of the book I'm once again trying to give a comprehensive account of values education: first by noting in Chapter 12 a variety of ways in which adults learn values; then by outlining in the present chapter a range of educational approaches; and finally by mentioning in Chapter 14 some additional components of sound values education. Once again I won't succeed, but I hope the horizon will have been usefully extended.

Faced with the great breadth of the field of values education, we should resist the tendency either to despair or to retreat into a sharp division of labor. Despair isn't called for, because we humans are capable of handling very complex tasks and are already solving many problems rather well. Neither is narrow specialization appropriate because, as Buckminster Fuller argued in *Operating Manual for Spaceship Earth*, the more we are involved in neighboring areas, the better we are able to find solutions in the areas we have chosen for special attention.

If all this is true, it follows that individual theorists and practitioners of values education shouldn't see themselves as able single-handedly to meet people's value needs or provide all the answers. Rather we are helping in a total process, much of which was already in place before we arrived and much of which is being guided anyhow by the learners themselves (as individuals and in groups). However, we can make a very important *contribution*, especially if we have a comprehensive view of the field, extend our efforts as broadly as possible, and link up with others around us.

CHAPTER 14

Learning and Teaching Values Through Dialogue

We have looked at how adults learn values (Chapter 12) and at traditional and modern approaches to adult values education (Chapter 13). In this way, we have reviewed many of the elements of values learning and teaching. In the present chapter, building on the previous two but going beyond them, I will suggest some new emphases for the future. My particular focus will be on *dialogue* as a key component of values education.

While stressing dialogue, I don't wish to suggest that is all there is to values education, or that I am proposing as an alternative "the dialogical approach." We saw in the previous chapter how comprehensive values education must be, and discussion is only part of process. However, the concept of dialogue captures much of what, in my view, has been lacking in values education in modern times. Also, the role of dialogue is currently being widely discussed by philosophers, theologians, sociologists, feminist theorists, and others, and it is appropriate that values educators and everyday learners should take advantage of the insights being developed.

Genuine Dialogue

As indicated in several earlier chapters, a major problem in values education today is its authoritarian, "top-down" quality. One way to overcome this is to ensure that values learning takes place through dialogue, rather than by teachers telling learners how to live.

A model of learning through dialogue has been proposed by a number of contemporary thinkers, notably Paulo Freire, Jürgen Habermas, and (following Habermas) Jack Mezirow and Seyla Benhabib.[1] These writers have roots in the Continental "hermeneutic" school of thought, which emphasizes respect for people's ongoing form of life and change through "discourse" within a tradition rather than by external imposition. However, they have added to the hermeneutic approach in various ways, in particular by stressing the need for dialogue *across* traditions.

Key aspects of the dialogue model are: (a) respect for each other's insights; (b) respect for each other's tradition or "story"; (c) freedom of speech, belief, action; (d) shared control of the form and content of dialogue; (e) focus on concrete, lived experience; and (f) testing through action ("praxis").

We educators often *claim* to respect the ideas and traditions of our students, but in fact largely ignore them and impose our own structure and content. It's not unheard of, for example, for a professor to give a two-

1. This is a somewhat arbitrary selection. I refer to Mezirow especially because of his contribution to the field of adult education. Benhabib, though a relatively junior member of the group, is mentioned because she has given a singularly clear and reflective analysis of Habermas's position, and also provides a link with feminist thought.

hour lecture on the importance of dialogue! *Use* of dialogue, as distinct from talking about it, compels us to practise what we preach by building mutual help and respect into the structure of inquiry. As Habermas says, it is only through "an actually carried out discourse" that the necessary "*exchange of roles* of each with every other (is) forced upon us."[2]

Even with a dialogue format, however, authoritarianism may continue. Careful planning and constant vigilance are needed to ensure that learners indeed have freedom of speech, belief, and action and the influence is reciprocal. Benhabib points out how constraints on learners may be built into the very language we use and the structure of our institutions. She speaks of:

> . . . those social relations, power structures, and socio-cultural grids of communication and interpretation . . . which limit the identity of the parties to the dialogue, which set the agenda for what is considered appropriate or inappropriate matter of institutional debate, and which sanctify the speech of some over those of others as being the language of the public.[3]

She insists, therefore, that not only must we "recognize the right of all beings capable of speech and action to be participants in the moral conversation"; but also, within such conversation, each person must have "the same symmetrical rights to various speech acts, to initiate new topics, to ask for reflection about the presuppositions of

2. Quoted in S. White, *The Recent Work of Jürgen Habermas* (Cambridge: Cambridge University Press, 1988), p. 73.
3. S. Benhabib, "In the Shadow of Aristotle and Hegel: Communicative Ethics and Current Controversies in Practical Philosophy," in *Hermeneutics and Critical Theory in Ethics and Politics*, ed. M. Kelly (Cambridge, Mass.: MIT Press, 1990), p. 19.

the conversation, etc." In Benhabib's view, these conditions of genuine dialogue are implicit in Habermas's description of an "ideal speech situation."[4] Learners must not only have the opportunity to speak but also share control over the form and content of the dialogue.

Emphasis on concrete, lived experience is also crucial to the dialogue model. Without it learners understand little of what is being said, and also feel they have little to contribute. This doesn't mean that theory should be absent: as we saw in Chapter 12, theory is crucial in values learning. However, much of the theory must be generated by the learners themselves; and theory introduced from other sources must be relevant to the learners' past, present, and likely future experience. In everyday life, we don't normally start up a conversation with someone and then proceed to talk about matters remote from their own experience and of no interest to them; and the same should hold true in dialogical values education.

Finally, according to Freire, Habermas, and others, dialogue must take place in the context of action. Value inquiry must proceed by means of "praxis," a combination of reflection and action. This is necessary both to ensure that the questions being pursued are indeed important, and to provide a means of validating proposed answers. Praxis deepens the partnership by ensuring that participants in the dialogue are not only talking to each other but also engaged in joint life projects. It also underscores the point that dialogue is impossible except in the context of a way of life that is at least to some degree shared. Women and men, for example, or adults and children, can't dialogue if they live quite separate lives.

4. *Ibid.*, pp. 6-7.

A "Hermeneutic" Approach

As noted, the contemporary emphasis on dialogue is in part due to the impact of the hermeneutic movement in Continental philosophy. The word "hermeneutic" comes from the Greek *hermeneutikos* meaning "interpretation." A hermeneutic approach is one in which the tradition, narrative, or story of an individual or group is respected and cherished, being seen as something to be interpreted and understood rather than roughly pushed aside by "objective," "scientific" inquiry (in pejorative senses of these terms).

A hermeneutic, dialogical approach is incremental in nature. As we saw in Chapters 1 and 12, once we accept that there is much that is good in people's present way of life, we see values education as "fine-tuning" rather than replacement. We enter into dialogue with people so we can (with them) interpret their way of life and, with that understanding, work out (with them) what modifications are needed. This doesn't imply an ideologically conservative approach. The modifications developed may be quite "drastic" and "radical" from certain points of view: they may even involve "revolutions" or "conversions." But they will still be incremental from the point of view of the total, multifaceted way of life which remains largely intact at any given time.

An assumption of the hermeneutic approach is that a tradition or life story is largely (some would say only) understood from within. We "interpret a tradition from within a tradition";[5] interpretation of a tradition or way of life goes in a "hermeneutic circle": "there is nothing beyond the unfolding text itself to which an appeal can be

5. T. Kisiel, "The Happening of Tradition: the Hermeneutics of Gadamer and Heidegger," in *Hermeneutics and Praxis*, ed. R. Hollinger (Notre Dame, Ind.: University of Indiana Press, 1985), p.5.

made."[6] This makes the need for dialogue clear: it's absurd to try to tell people how they should live without understanding their present way of life and the reasons for it. We must engage in dialogue to understand their narrative and (together) work out how to modify its future direction as necessary.

I have spoken of "our" entering into dialogue with "them" to establish the future direction of "their" way of life. However, this way of putting it can leave open the door to authoritarianism. In fact, in *genuine* dialogue, the influence of them (the "learners") on us (the "teachers") is just as important, so the distinction between learners and teachers becomes problematic. We will examine this issue more closely later.

I said above that in the hermeneutic, dialogical approach we aren't "objective" and "scientific," but rather understand a way of life from within. However, I was using these terms in a pejorative sense. In fact, I believe there is an important sense in which hermeneutic inquiry — and values dialogue — *should* be objective and scientific. As we saw in Chapter 2, basic human values are embedded in human nature and can be objectively studied, as can the conditions under which various goods are attained. The basic, intermediate, and specific values change to some extent with time and context, but these changes too can be monitored. Part of the point of a hermeneutic, dialogical method, then, is to achieve a more subtle, accurate grasp of people's actual or *objective* circumstances and needs. Such an approach is more — rather than less — *scientific* than others commonly used, while not being "objective" or "scientific" in the pejorative sense of ignoring people's inner life and concrete situation.

6. W. Feinberg and J. Soltis, *School and Society* (New York: Teachers College Press, 1985), p. 96.

There is always the danger with a hermeneutic approach of slipping into relativism; of denying objectivity and defining knowledge in terms of our ideas (or those of our community). In saying that value inquiry and dialogue must (in a sense) be objective and scientific, I'm rejecting a relativist approach. The issues here are of course ancient and difficult. However, while our *beliefs* about life and reality may be true or false, *knowledge* is by definition true (even though we probably can never know for certain what is true). We must always distinguish between understanding the beliefs of an individual or group and assessing the (objective) truth or validity of those beliefs. Although our perception of what we know keeps changing, the distinction between belief and knowledge is nevertheless crucial.

"Teachers" and "Students" Learning Together

In genuine dialogue, the learning is two-way. It is not authoritarian or "top-down." Teachers aren't in general considered superior in their values to learners. In line with our discussion in Chapters 6 and 7, we don't distinguish between "higher stage" teachers and "lower stage" learners.

Sometimes a values teacher appears to be exceptionally wise in a wide range of value matters. However, this is sometimes true of learners, too, if they have the opportunity to express their wisdom. Also, this is an unusual occurrence: typically values teachers and learners alike show only a modest degree of wisdom. And, more importantly, even where a teacher has superior wisdom in some areas, learners have superior wisdom in other areas, and the question of who knows more about what is open-ended so it's rather petty to try to calculate who is the values "champion." Assuming that values learning is largely problem-centred (as advocated in Chapter 12), each issue and sub-topic should be approached afresh, without preconceptions about who will be able to contribute the most.

The illusion that teachers are wiser than learners in value matters has been sustained over the centuries not only by phase and stage notions and age-ist prejudices, but also by the way values teaching has been structured. Teachers have controlled the agenda, dwelling on concepts and issues (often largely academic) with which they are familiar, and keeping the discussion away from the rich insights of ordinary people. Students have done well or poorly in debates and tests depending on their interest in and mastery of the *teacher's* subject matter. We have had a sense of teaching a great deal to our students and learning very little from them, which has reinforced our sense of superiority; but what we have mainly done is teach students our notions about values and test their recall of these (largely inert) ideas. They have in fact learned little; and we, by avoiding their areas of competence, have missed an opportunity to learn much.

By contrast, what I'm proposing is that "teachers and students learn together," each sharing insights with the others. This requires a radical shift in subject matter, so people's *real* life problems (and areas of experience) are explored; but obviously that is all to the good. It was always bizarre that the *learners* (for whose benefit — supposedly — the exercise was arranged) should have had their attention focussed on the *teachers'* interests. As has been observed, education often becomes a matter of teachers asking questions of students, when if anything it should be the other way round. But ideally values education should be a dialogue in which teachers and learners ask each other questions, so *both* are teachers and learners.

Would such a change of agenda place teachers in a difficult and unpleasant position? In some ways perhaps so, especially in the short-run; but I believe that on balance and in the long-run, the teachers' situation would be considerably improved. On the one hand, learners would be much more appreciative of teachers' efforts; and on the other hand, teachers would learn much more about values, since they would be able to draw systematically on the wealth of experience and insight of learners. Teaching would be a much more rewarding activity, in terms of both the teachers' own growth and their relationship with their "students."

Is any room left, then, for the distinction between "teachers" and "learners," if all are in fact learning together in dialogue? We will examine this question in the next section, after considering Freire's views on the role of "revolutionary leaders."

The Role of the "Teacher"

If values teaching is dialogical and reciprocal, if teachers and students learn *together*, is there any place left for "teachers"? This question is seldom seriously addressed even by advocates of dialogue, who often are rather domineering teachers. Paulo Freire, for example, is at best unclear on this issue, and may be seen as remaining authoritarian in some respects, valuable though his account is.

In *Pedagogy of the Oppressed*,[7] Freire states:

> Through dialogue, the teacher-of-the-students and the students-of-the-teacher cease to exist and a new term emerges: teacher-student with student-teachers. The teacher is no longer merely the one-who-teaches, but one who is . . . taught in dialogue with the students, who in turn while being taught also teach. They become jointly responsible for a

7. P. Freire, *Pedagogy of the Oppressed*, transl. M. Bergman Ramos (New York: Herder and Herder, 1972; originally 1968). All references in this chapter are to this volume.

> process in which all grow. In this process, arguments based on "authority" are no longer valid . . . . Here, no one teaches another, nor is anyone self-taught. (People) teach each other. (p. 67)[8]

Freire quotes with approval Mao Tse-tung's dictums:

> . . . we must teach to the masses clearly what we have received from them confusedly. (p. 82)
>
> . . . All work done for the masses must start from their needs and not from the desire of any individual, however well-intentioned. . . . There are two principles here: one is the actual needs of the masses rather than what we fancy they need, and the other is the wishes of the masses, who must make up their own minds instead of our making up their minds for them. (p. 83)

Nevertheless, Freire continues to speak of teachers and of revolutionary leaders. He states that the dialogical theory of action

> . . . does not mean that in the dialogical task there is no role for revolutionary leadership. It means merely that the leaders — in spite of their important, fundamental, and indispensable role — do not own the people and have no right to steer the people blindly towards their salvation. (p. 167)

The role of the revolutionary leader is one of "cultural synthesis" rather than "cultural invasion."

> In cultural synthesis, the actors who came from "another world" to the world of the people do so not as invaders. They do not come to *teach* or to

8. In this quotation I have deleted or changed non-inclusive language.

> *transmit* or to *give* anything, but rather to learn with the people, about the people's world. (p. 181)

Freire further specifies the role of revolutionary leaders:

> In this synthesis, leaders and people are somehow reborn in new knowledge and new action. . . . The more sophisticated knowledge of the leaders is remade in the empirical knowledge of the people, while the latter is refined by the former. (p. 183)
>
> Cultural synthesis . . . does not mean that the objectives of revolutionary action should be limited by the aspirations expressed in the world view of the people. If this were to happen (in the guise of respect for that view), the revolutionary leaders would be passively bound to that vision. Neither invasion by the leaders of the people's world view nor mere adaptation by the leaders to the (often naïve) aspirations of the people is acceptable. (p. 184)

Although Freire's discussion makes an enormous contribution, I feel it still involves some difficulties. Teachers/leaders are still too much set apart; and the extent and nature of what *they* have to learn is not acknowledged sufficiently. There is still a hint of general superiority and authority, as evidenced by his reference to their "more sophisticated knowledge" and the "often naïve" aspirations of the masses. Freire says that while the leaders must have confidence in the people,

> This confidence should not, however, be naïve. The leaders . . . must always mistrust the *ambiguity* of oppressed (people), mistrust the oppressor "housed" in the latter. (p. 169)
>
> . . . as long as the oppressor "within" the oppressed is stronger than they themselves are, their natural fear of freedom may lead them to denounce the

> revolutionary leaders instead! The leaders cannot be credulous, but must be alert for these possibilities. Guevara's [book] *Episodes* confirms these risks: not only desertions, but even betrayal of the cause. (pp. 169-70)

While there is some truth in these observations, they don't show sufficient recognition of the equally deep inadequacies in the "leaders." Further, certain general insights which are ascribed to the teachers/leaders — into the evils of inequality, the necessity of liberation, and the importance of "the cause," for example — are taken as givens, not open for discussion. One has the sense that the role of dialogue is to clothe the "sophisticated" liberation program of the leaders in the empirical details of local conditions, which of course only the local people can supply. It isn't envisaged that the program itself may be fundamentally changed by what the people have to say, that the leaders may encounter basic and *legitimate* disagreement about how to live, how to run a society, how to promote human well-being, what constitutes human well-being.

It is precisely this sense of the *extensive* and *fundamental* learning needs of so-called values "teachers" that is crucial to dialogue. So long as teachers don't recognize that their need is as great as that of their students, genuine dialogue won't be possible. Teachers must fully accept that we are all in the same boat, we are all members of a society and culture with problems that afflict everyone. Teachers must accept (as we saw in Chapter 7) that a society advances together — young and old, rich and poor, females and males, learners and teachers — rather than by one group running ahead and then helping the others catch up to them.

But why, then, continue to talk of "teachers" and "learners" in value matters? In my view, the distinction signals not a difference in value wisdom, but rather a difference in (a) professional role and (b) specific skills. Teachers of values are designated (and often paid) to create and implement programs of values learning, both formal and informal; and they acquire (or have naturally) special skills in facilitating values learning. However, the programs they create are *for themselves as much as for their "students"*; indeed, if they aren't constantly learning themselves, they hinder the learning of others. Further, while they are the ones "in charge" of the learning program, one of their responsibilities is to help ensure that the "learners" have a major teaching role and a major say in what form the program takes. In a very real sense, they are the servants of the learners.

A values teacher might be compared in certain respects to a sporting coach. A hockey coach, for example, may not be able to play as well as *any* of the members of the team and yet have outstanding coaching skills and be highly valued. Being a good coach certainly requires various insights and abilities, but not necessarily greater playing ability. It may happen on occasion that a coach *is* a better player than all the team members; just as occasionally values teachers may be wiser on average than their students (although never in every area). But such general superiority is by no means essential to being an excellent coach or teacher.

In their professional role, values teachers often have very considerable authority. They are usually the ones designated to draw up an initial topic outline and reading list, make sure certain resources are available, assign grades to class members, and so on. There is enormous room for abuse here; and given the traditions of teaching and learning in our society, it's extremely difficult to avoid authoritarianism completely. However, the *ideal* should remain non-authoritarian and dialogical; and teachers should do everything they can to *serve* their students, working *with* them to ensure that genuine dialogue takes place.

The Importance of Content

Values dialogue without content, without "grist for the mill," is largely a waste of time. Some have referred to it as "pooling of ignorance." Others have called it "quandary ethics," where people sit around wondering what the right and the good could possibly be, when in fact we all have strong views on the subject.

In Chapter 12 I argued that *instruction* is crucial to values learning: people need information about value theories; about the consequences of particular actions; about alternative ways of achieving their goals; about alternative ways of viewing the world and approaching life. In Chapter 13 I claimed that other approaches to values education must be supplemented by *direct* values teaching. The emphasis on dialogue in this chapter is not meant as a retraction of these claims. Content of these kinds is essential. Rather the point is that learners as well as teachers should make a substantial input into the discussion, and should have a say in what information and ideas are made available as a basis for dialogue. Teachers shouldn't use their role as "the instructor" to control the topics and resources of a learning group or to dominate the dialogue. As outlined in Chapter 13, what is needed is a new concept of "instruction," according to which students teach teachers (and each other) as well as vice versa.

Participants in a dialogue — both "teachers" and "students" — should state strongly and in detail what they value and why. They should engage in "value advocacy." Without such input, people will learn little, and participants will wonder why the dialogue is taking place at all. It is important to show one's seriousness about values. The way to avoid indoctrination is not to refrain from expressing a point of view but rather, while doing so, to allow others to express their views, listen to them carefully, and be ready to change one's own views in light of the discussion.

Even the "banking" or "storage" of ideas is often legitimate. Freire has argued strongly and largely convincingly against a "banking" concept of education, where learners are viewed merely as receptacles in which knowledge is stored for future use. He rightly insists that learners must be actively involved in their education, and not simply have something done *to* them over which they have no control. However, we have all had the experience of making use of a concept or piece of information acquired with little comprehension on an earlier occasion and being glad that we now have it at our disposal. Even in genuine dialogue many things are said (by teachers *and* fellow learners) which we don't understand at the time but which prove invaluable in later life. Once again, the point about dialogue is not that such banking shouldn't occur but rather that all participants should have equal privileges in making deposits (so to speak!), in determining what ideas and information the group is exposed to.

Dialogue, then, isn't "discovery learning" in the sense that teachers give no hint of what they value or why and students are expected to discover everything for themselves from scratch. That is a singularly ineffective way to teach and learn, at best too individualistic and lonely and at worst a subtle form of indoctrination where teachers let students gradually find out what they (the teachers) already are certain of (a kind of "timed-release" form of teaching). "Discovery learning" is the antithesis of dialogue since it doesn't involve people seriously talking with each other. Admittedly, there is always a major element of original discovery in learning; but students and teachers alike learn much more if they have the benefit of extensive input — what I have called "content" — from each other and from other sources.

At this point, I would suggest that the reader look at the sample study units in Chapter 11, and consider how these could be used in genuine dialogue. They certainly illustrate how a teacher (myself, in this case) might have strong input into a discussion, proposing certain values and the reasons for them. But what steps would be needed to ensure that learners had equally strong input into the form and content of the discussion, so that authoritarianism and indoctrination could as far as possible be avoided?

To end, let me repeat the invitation to readers given in the Introduction to approach this book as the beginning of a dialogue rather than a finished product. I would like to practise what I've preached about dialogue. I would be very glad to hear your views about values, adult development, learning, teaching, and any of the other topics we've been discussing, so that I can learn from you.

Index